CHALLENGED TO CHANGE

A true story of a victim's journey to victory

Change your attitude change your life

CHERYL J. FOSTER, M.A. ASSOCIATE MINISTER

PHOTOGRAPHY BY: LUTHER FOSTER, JR.

Lousphotography888@att.net

Photography by Luther Foster, Jr.
Lousphotography888@att.net

Editor: Shann Hall-LochmannVanBennekom

Interior Designer: Tony Bradford

Front Cover Designer: Dionne Preston

Back Cover Designer: Robert King

ISBN: 978-1-938950-47-6

Greater Is He Publishing
9824 E. Washington St.
Chagrin Falls, Ohio 44023
Phone: 216.288.9315
www.GreaterIsHePublishing.com

DEDICATION

I dedicate this book to my Lord God and Savior, Jesus Christ, who I want to please daily.

St. John 10:10* reads, "The thief cometh not, but for to steal, and to kill, and to destroy: I am come that they might have life, and that they might have it more abundantly."

I dedicate this book to my faithful, loving husband and soul mate, Luther Foster, Jr., I love you, dear.

I dedicate this book to the late O'Dell Nelson, my father, whom I love and miss. Dad, thanks for every lesson.

I dedicate this book to the late, Honorable Bishop Norman L. Wagner, my spiritual father, whom I love and respect.

I dedicate this book to Suffragan Bishop C. Shawn Tyson, my pastor, and the Calvary Ministries International Church family. Love and thanks to you.

I dedicate this book to Yvonne D. Wagner, Miss Tel-a-World. Thanks for promoting my books. I honor your memory.

I dedicate this to everyone who gave written, spoken, and encouraging input, identified by his or her contributions throughout the book.

ACKNOWLEDGEMENTS

Mama Nelson, I love you. I call you *blessed.* Love, from your oldest child.

Mom Foster shared her ninety years of wisdom prior to God calling her home. I hold every gem close to my heart.

Aaron Thomason, my nephew, thanks and love for throwing me a L.I.F.E. line when I was drowning in the sea of adversity. Ebonique, we thank you for lending Aaron to us for this season.

To my daughter, Juanita La Shawn, and granddaughters, Maya Cherie, LaKina, and Loneeka thanks with love.

My spiritual daughters, Claudette, Hattie, Taunita, Annette, Marnie, and Portia; I thank you for building the team in love.

Pastor Yvonne Hawkins-Bell, Bishop Harry S. Grayson, Bishop Willie Thornton, Ministers Regina, Nancy, Katrina, Vivian, Ivy, Jewell, Ruby, Belinda, Brenda, Ann, Sarah, and numerous friends who supported me in ministry and L.I.F.E.; your gifts of friendship are priceless.

Jon Scallia and Dustin Hall, you are sensitive and gifted YSU English instructors and tutors. The YSU Writing Center is a valuable resource for making dreams come true. Thank you.

Dawson, a very effective and innovative therapist, taught us the Psychology of Intimate Relationships. Thank you for allowing me to participate as a student with skills and experience. The respect will always be mutual.

Special thanks to a special editor, Shann, my midwife who helped me learn to surrender and labor in an excellent way.

Attending YSU Metro College Over-Sixty Program has given me the opportunity to bridge the generation gap. Thank You.

Betty Oliver, you brought me the leopard butterfly, on the right day, at the right time and God only knows how much you impact my life. I love you, Friend.

Jewell Finley was a champion who has defied all odds. She was an absolute miracle; she always gave God great glory. When we see Jesus, we are looking forward to hearing her testimony about receiving help from the Lord.

Over one hundred former team members and sponsors have fostered community growth, development, and life to the valley. THANK YOU.

TABLE OF CONTENTS

INTRODUCTION 1

CHAPTER 1—CHALLENGED TO LOVE: LOVE IS
                THE MASTER KEY 5

CHAPTER 2—CHALLENGED TO LIVE THE
                ABUNDANT LIFE: OBEDIENCE
                IS THE KEY 33

CHAPTER 3—CHALLENGED TO TAKE A STEP
                BEYOND: WALK ON BY FAITH 58

CHAPTER 4—CHALLENGED TO IMAGINE:
                DREAMS OR NIGHTMARES 89

CHAPTER 5—CHALLENGED TO BE RISEN BY
                DECISION: ADVERSITY IS THE
                FATHER OF MENTAL TOUGHNESS... 113

CHAPTER 6—CHALLENGED TO BELIEVE THIS
                IS A BLESSING: I'M TOO BLESSED
                TO BE STRESSED 138

CHAPTER 7—CHALLENGED TO CHOOSE:
                THERE ARE TWO OF YOU 164

CHAPTER 8—CHALLENGED TO CHANGE: FROM
                IMMATURITY TO MATURITY 179

CHAPTER 9— CHALLENGED TO CHANGE WHEN
                GOD REVEALS TO HEAL:
                FLIP THE SCRIPT 202

CHAPTER 10— CHALLENGED TO CHANGE
WHEN WINDOWS OF OPPORTUNITY
OPEN: SEE JESUS 223

INTRODUCTION

Two of the most important dates in your life are the day you are born and the day you discover who you are. *Challenged to Change* is a life-saver designed for everyone who wants to improve their quality and longevity of life for themselves and others. This book is also for those who feel they are living beneath their privilege and desire to live the life they were meant to live. My hope for you is, after reading this book, you'll understand that no matter where or who you are right now, when you end your journey, you'll not only be in a different place, but you'll be a totally different person.

As a native of Detroit, Michigan, once known as *The Murder Capital of the World,* I graduated from the Detroit Public Schools. Life in the city taxed, challenged, and awed me.

I moved to Ypsilanti, Michigan, and attended Eastern Michigan University. While attending the university, I went through a divorce, became a single parent, and transitioned to remain in

Ypsilanti, Michigan, which is a rural environment, quite the contrast from Detroit.

As a senior in college, one of my male classmates and I were studying Sociology when he said, "Cheryl, why don't we exchange your African Album for my book, *The Power of Positive Thinking,* by Norman Vincent Peale?"

"Sure, why not; I love to read." The impact of this book provided long-term changes and helped me fulfill long-forgotten dreams and goals. Reading the positive-thinking principles eventually led me to change from attending church occasionally to becoming a regular member of an unfamiliar church culture. I was eventually born of the water and spirit. Yes, I am born again!

My journey started as an immature Christian, moving from victim to victor. This process required me to change my heart and my mind, to refuse to allow Satan to creep into my thought process. I needed to redirect my path and follow Jesus' footsteps. These first steps were the driving force of my journey. Philippians 1:6* states, "Being confident of this very thing, that He which hath begun a good work in you will perform it until the day of Jesus Christ."

As long as you are still drawing breath, it's never too late to change, and you are never too old to accept Jesus and begin your new life in Him. The words of "The Serenity Prayer," by Reinhold Niebuhr, have helped me get through many difficult times. I often find myself asking God to give me the ability to make the changes I need to make in order to live the life Jesus wants for me. Sometimes, I need to pray for strength to accept things that I cannot change. Then, of course, there is always the fine line between the two; that's when I ask God for the wisdom I need in order to live according to His Will.

I also find comfort in the Bible. Proverbs 3:5-6 is God responding to me in a clear and concise way. I keep this prayer close to my heart and flip to it often to obtain, maintain, and sustain a focused and intentional life with significance. I am not *writing* this book, but paving the way for us by *praying* this book into print.

"Trust in the Lord with all thine heart; and lean not unto thine own understanding. In all thy ways acknowledge him, and he shall direct thy paths." (Proverbs 3:5-6)

CHAPTER 1

CHALLENGED TO LOVE:
LOVE IS THE MASTER KEY

Love is the master key to unlock your purpose in life. Learning to love is a life-long journey, where you'll learn that walking hand in hand with Jesus makes the walk easier. God is love. When it comes to life and love, there are always questions that pop up. Who am I? Am I lovable, likeable, or tolerable? Can I love others like Jesus loves me? What exactly does love look like? Can I change and make this love part of my life? What does this Godly love cost me? Am I *willing* to change in order to appreciate God's love fully?

I answered the last question with a hearty, "Yes! I accept the challenge to love." Remember, whenever you decide to initiate change, you will be tested on your conviction and commitment.

Approximately eight years ago, during the Women's Ecclesia Staff meeting, Evangelist Sherri

Brogdon so aptly expounded on love as she presented the theme for 2006: "A Heart to Serve, *Love is the Master Key.*" This topic was based on Deuteronomy 10:12, "And now, Israel, what doth the Lord thy God require of thee, but to fear the Lord thy God, to walk in all His ways, and to love Him, and to serve the Lord thy God with all thy heart and with all thy soul."

Placing her hand on my shoulder, she looked me in the eye as she spoke. "Cheryl, one day God's going to bless you to work in a ministry of love."

I shook my head and laughed. "Oh, Sherri, I find that hard to believe. Right now, my life is full of haters, and I don't know how to love someone who is filled with such hate."

Her words stuck with me though, and I remember pondering in my heart her prophetic utterance.

One question kept coming up whenever I reflected on her words. "Am I a loving, likeable person?" I needed to find that answer. I poured through my Bible and God spoke to me through the words found in Matthew 22:37-40. "Jesus said unto him, 'Thou shalt love The Lord Thy God with all thy heart, and with all thy soul, and with all thy mind. This is the first great commandment. And the second is like unto it, Thou shalt love thy neighbor as thyself. On these two commandments hang all the law of the prophets.' "

Since the Bible clearly states that God is love and that He commands us to fulfill the Law of Love, I realized that in God's eyes I am loveable. I may not always deserve His love, but He loves me unconditionally. This law reflects God's character. As Christians, we mirror His character when we love those who He created in His image. Love provides the foundation of everything good.

WHAT IS LOVE?

In order to start on the journey that God has planned for you, it's important first to understand the meaning of the word *love*. It's one of the smaller words in the English language, and yet it is one of the hardest to define. *The Merriam-Webster*

Dictionary states that love is "strong affection for another arising out of kinship or personal ties." Therefore, we often define love by the way we feel or as a feeling.

Love is not a feeling; it is a set of behaviors and choices. Love is a commitment. It is a difficult word to define conceptually. In 1 John 4:7-8, we are told, "Beloved, let us love one another: for love is of God: and every one that loveth is born of God, and knoweth God. He, who loveth not, knoweth not God; for God is love." This means that everyone who has ever truly loved someone must know God because God is love. Likewise, if you do not love someone, you cannot claim to know God. God has a fatherly love for humanity. God's love seems intangible, something we cannot touch, taste, see, hear, feel or smell, but He is the source of all love. You must love everyone because God loves all people.

Love is the very essence of God's nature. He sent Jesus to be the peacemaker between your sinful self and the Father. Loving God and trusting Him implicitly removes all fears from your heart. God is the first object of your love. If you love God, you must love others. You can't separate the two because God is love. If you claim truly to love God, then your heart needs to be open to loving all of His children as well. Your goal, as a Christian, is to love in the same way Jesus loves you. It's important to be respectful to yourself while you love others in order to avoid a love deficit. Love is balanced and all-inclusive; it excludes no one, not even you.

I believe low self-esteem hurts God immensely. He created you and loves you; therefore, it hurts Him when you are unable to love yourself. You need to learn to repent from the state of self-abuse and begin to progress to the ultimate dimension of love.

Four Greek words that define different degrees of love in the Bible are *Eros*, an erotic love; *Phileo,* brotherly love; *Storge*, family love; and *Agape*, the highest form of love, God's love.

You begin your journey by making one change at a time. The first challenge is to compare human, conditional love to God's divine, unconditional love. Some may find it difficult to receive God's love, even though others might find it easy. Many people make the mistake of believing that they must live up to all of God's expectations. If they are unable to do so, then feelings of worthlessness may creep in because their perception of God's love is the same as human or performance-based love.

God wants you to receive His love. On one level or another, everyone hungers for love because it is a basic need for all humans. God uses pain as one of His master tools in developing maturity. If you fail to discard outdated, childish behaviors, it's almost impossible to love in a mature fashion. You develop unconditional love when you learn new skill sets during transitions and passages in life.

The best representation of God's love for you is seen through His horrific pain and sacrifice on the cross. Crucifixion is one of the most excruciating ways to murder another human. Jesus knew what lay ahead of Him, yet still he endured the torture, the humiliation, and the betrayal because of his love for you. When I say you, I mean it personally. If you were the only person Jesus would save by dying on the cross, He still would have endured it all because He loves you that much. The passion of Christ exemplifies love at its best. He loves you, which enables you to love others, including yourself. If you don't possess love, then you can't give it to others.

St. John 3:16 reads, "For God so loved the world that He gave His only begotten Son, that whosoever believeth in Him should not perish, but have everlasting life." God made the choice to love when he created the universe and everything in it. His love, and only His love, is without limits. You complete God's love by choosing to have an intimate relationship with Him. You are the benefactor from Jesus' death by receiving life and having the ultimate relationship with Him.

God's pattern is the only one you should emulate. Love is many things; it is a choice and a commitment. Love is not passive. It requires action. It's about caring for others, even someone who has hurt you. It's not about you anymore. Once you choose to receive God's love, you move past the basics into a higher realm, knowing God is able to do anything.

Whenever you have to make a choice, you have a talk with yourself; you weigh the pros and cons. Your soul is comprised of your mind, will, and emotions, so it must be in proper alignment in order to process the information directly from your spirit.

Once God sends the message to love with all your heart, this message is deposited into your spirit. Your spirit transfers the message to the transmitter, also known as your soul. If your soul dispatches the message from a pure heart and unconditional love, your spirit connects with the Spirit of God; then, you will surpass the natural thought patterns and human behaviors, responding in obedience. Some people only obey the Bible verses that they believe. You must learn how to believe *all* of the Scriptures and do what God says.

God created people for a special purpose. He wants you to love Him. One way to show this love is to care for others and show the people in your life God's unconditional love. Another way to fulfill your purpose is to obey God's laws. This means it's important to read the Bible and to understand what He is saying to you. Some people only obey certain verses, but that isn't pleasing to God. If you find yourself doubting aspects of the Bible or not fully understanding certain verses, the first thing you should do is pray for strength and wisdom. Sometimes, it's easier to think, *God didn't mean me when He said this.* One important verse to remember when making the decision to love is Romans 13:10. "Love does no harm to our neighbor; therefore, love is the fulfillment of the law."

When you don't recognize God's love for you, it can become easy to find you are suddenly filled with hatred, bitterness, and bad intentions. Forgiving others may not be on your list of priorities. At times like this, it's important to identify the matters of the heart. Ephesians 4:2

instructs you to be humble, gentle, patient, and to treat others with love.

At one point in my life, my heart was filled with negative feelings and thoughts. I found myself doing things that shamed me. No longer was I the person most likely to succeed. Instead, I became a victim, and then, a survivor of domestic violence. According to statistics, life didn't look very promising. Some studies show twenty-six people, most likely females, will be assaulted by their partners every fifteen minutes. Roughly, every two to three days, six women will be killed by a violent partner. The numbers increase dramatically if you extend the survey to the entire world, with likely hundreds of women dying a violent death in a short time.

After years of living with a violent man, I experienced the residue of the abnormal misuse or abuse that left me spiritually, physically, emotionally, and financially challenged as a newborn Christian.

I remember God's miraculous love when my daughter, Juanita La Shawn, and my lives were spared. We were in the house when her father went into a rage. Benny had grabbed an axe, and suddenly, he started swinging and chopping at anything in his path. As soon as I spotted an opportunity, I whispered in my daughter's ear, "When Daddy goes in the next room, I want you to quietly creep out the back door, and then, run to the neighbor's for help."

Even though her eyes were filling with tears and she jumped every time a crash echoed in her ears, she nodded her head.

I held my breath, waiting for the right time. When it came, I nodded at Juanita LaShawn. She stood up on trembling legs, hugged the wall, and escaped out the door. Benny literally destroyed everything in the apartment. I saw wood flying from the broken furniture; glass tables and shelves were shattered; mud was slung on our yellow walls and carpet from the soil in the plants. The mud permanently damaged our beautiful carpet. I was in

shock, too numb to speak. I could only pray silently.
Thank God for the Blood.

My thoughts were twisted and I could only focus on the negative aspects. It took years for me to fully understand how that painful, emotional experience allowed me to gather the strength I needed to change my situation. At first, I wasn't sure if God would be able to change my heart permanently. Even after time had gone by, I found bits of anger and resentment creeping back in. Today, I've learned to appreciate the challenges in my life because of the beautiful lessons and examples of Jesus' love for me that are present in every difficult situation. I never overcame by myself; no, Jesus stayed with me along every step of my journey. He carried me through the hardest times because He loves me unconditionally. I've come to learn that God has created me for a special purpose. Currently, He is calling me to assist others who want to improve the quality of their own lives. Even though they are hurting, God has asked me to help them heal and teach them to do the work needed in order to live a happy and long life.

This change didn't happen overnight. It wasn't until my nineteen-year-old granddaughter, Maya Cherie, challenged me. One day, as we left the doctor's office, she put her hand on my arm and looked me in the eyes. "Grandma, I'm worried about you; all you do is go to doctors and hospitals or stay home. Don't you have a life anymore?"

Speechless, I pondered her words before responding. "Maya, I'm going to get a new life."

The law of attraction is a belief that states that every bad thing that has happened to you is a result of your own actions or decisions. It only makes sense then, that if you create the bad things in your life, you can also tear down the distasteful thoughts and create new ideas and plans. That day, walking home from the doctor with my granddaughter, I decided to use my God-given, creative ability to change.

Her question, asked in love for me, made me realize I had been living a stagnant life, stuck between two kingdoms, fatigue and compassion. After experiencing tremendous success in helping thousands of hurting people, I was hurting. I finally realized when helping others started hurting me that I needed to adjust and refocus.

I experienced horrific wear and tear and became too exhausted and stressed to love God, others, and even myself. I crashed and burned. I realized I'd put all my faith in others and didn't leave any for myself. My own deficiencies and feelings of inadequacy made me feel unqualified and unable to keep my promises. Until my granddaughter pointed this out to me, I'd been totally oblivious to my own state of mind.

You too may feel unworthy to serve God and others. Often, it can be easy to fall into the trap of thinking the way to please God is to follow your own heart and desires. In order to meet the approval of other people, you may discover that you start cutting out your personal time with God. This choice leads you to believe that your faith is based on your ability to perform many different functions.

God sends a message to your heart. Your heart may be decayed, as stated in Jeremiah 17:9-10. "The heart is deceitful above all things and desperately wicked: who can know it? I the Lord search the heart, I try the reins, even to give every man according to his ways, and according to the fruit of his doings." The soul misperceives the message, transmits the message using conditional love, and disconnects the message of divine love. The body perceives an improper message and reacts with negative, carnal, fleshly behavior.

You need to remember that God yearns for you to long for a relationship with Him. Believe it or not, you're not too different from some of the heroes from the Bible. King David repeatedly begged God not to hide His face or to be far away from him.

King David declares his intense longing for intimacy with God in Psalms 27:4. "One thing have I desired of the Lord, that will I seek after; that I may dwell in the house of the Lord all the days of my life, to behold the beauty of the Lord, and to inquire in His temple." David desired to be the center of God's heart. That's what a real relationship is all about.

As a Christian, your need to draw closer to God's presence is crucial because He really sees, knows, and cares about you. God is the one who plants the longing for belonging in your heart. The absence of being in the presence of God, however, may be based on your feelings of unworthiness of being blessed, which can result in low self-esteem.

During the busy time of my life, I began to miss my intimate time with God. I hungered for His love and found myself asking, "How do I draw nearer to God?" I had spent years of developing performing acts for the people of God, which ultimately, reduced my precious time in God's presence. At the time, I really thought I was doing the right thing for the right people in the right place, and in the right way. Soon, I discovered I actually was committing idolatry by trying to please man instead of God.

I became disillusioned with life. My nephew, Aaron, noticed that I, one of his role models in ministry, was struggling. Yet, for months, God whispered, "Remember, I've come to give you an abundant life." In my mind, I believed the abundant life Jesus was promising me meant that I was supposed to be busy, working every chance I had to minister to His people. Soon, I discovered God had another definition of an abundant life for me.

It was during this time when Aaron introduced me to L.I.F.E., a self-directed personal growth and leadership development program. Initially, I felt cautious, but soon curiosity took over. I decided to go to the source Himself. "God, is this you?"

Immediately after I enrolled in L.I.F.E., God used the program as a supplementary vehicle to get me out of the bed to continue the process on my spiritual journey. He resurrected dreams that had been lost, stolen, or forfeited. God revealed that the conditional love that I'd been experiencing was in direct contrast to His law.

The Law of Love can be found in Matthew 22:37-39. "Jesus said unto him, 'Thou shalt love the Lord thy God with all thy heart, and with all thy soul, and with all thy mind. This is the first and great commandment. And the second is like unto it, Thou shalt love thy neighbor as thyself.' "

Many people take this verse to mean you should love your neighbor more than you love yourself. God showed me that I was taking better care of others and loving them more than I loved myself. Something needed to change immediately. I realized I needed to love myself in order to understand the person that God created me to be. When God showed me His divine plan, I realized that He needed me to heal and restore myself in order to fulfill His conception.

One of L.I.FE.'s reading assignments described the different types of personalities. One of the older modules is called the Four Temperaments. Upon reading further, I identified my melancholy temperament as analytical, genius-prone, sensitive, deep, and gloomy. When I discovered that Moses,

Elijah, King David, and Jeremiah had suffered from melancholia, I was encouraged and hopeful.

You are the sum total of your environment, experiences, and genetic traits, which develop into your habits and characteristics. You need to learn how to love difficult people, including yourself. The first step is to realize that there are four distinct personalities, adversely positioned in four quadrants with four patterns. In the Bible, God uses a numeric system to explain many things. One example of the meaning of the number four is in the beginning of the Bible. On the fourth day, when God created the universe, He created the sun, the stars, and the moon, all of which divide day from night and one season from another. In other words, on the fourth day, God gave the world a sense of order. The unity and harmony of the Four Temperaments create a symphonic, Heavenly sound that garners God's attention and maintains His order in leadership.

You are a significant part of a team that needs your uniqueness. In order for me to remember that I, too, am unique and special in God's eyes, I begin my day with Psalms 118:24, "This is the day which the Lord hath made; we will rejoice and be glad in it." By actually saying those words every morning, I prepare myself to embrace each day as a special gift from God.

While reading another resource, God exposed some offenses I had embraced and allowed to turn into hidden hurts and fears. Hiding anger, a secondary emotion, results in toxic, reactionary relationships. God requires the accountability of the offended more than the offender. According to St. Luke 17:1-5, mature Christians trust God and give their offenses to Him, freeing God to deal with the offender on our behalf. In awe, I exclaimed, "Oh, my God, I repent!" I had blamed other people for the hurt I'd inflicted on myself by allowing others to mistreat me.

Eleanor Roosevelt stated, "No one can hurt you without your permission."

Orrin Woodward stated, "Results are inversely proportional to the level of self-deception; if you blame everyone else, how can you change for the better?"

This awareness allowed me to accept the challenge to move from existing in hate to living in love.

Taking up your cross and bearing it is a spiritual metaphor for what your flesh desires to avoid at all cost, which is to accept responsibility. Your cross would be that which requires you to sacrifice the people and things you love the most. You can't have it your way and still obey God's command, even if it's something you desire greatly.

Your cross might be that which you must bear alone in a public setting, while enduring private pain, in order to accomplish the perfect Will of God for your life. Your cross could be something that causes you pain while giving other people power. It's possible that bearing your cross means exposing all of your weaknesses and vulnerabilities to the world. Your cross could be the pivotal turning point in your life that determines the extent of your commitment to submit to the Will of God.

Love causes you to refuse to be offended. Love allows you to see the pain of those who have hurt you. When it seems easier to avoid the wounded people, go to them; don't pass them by. Show compassion and bind up their wounds, just as you would want others to show you compassion.

Love is the core and very essence of who you are and is designed to develop you as a loving, non-judgmental, worthwhile person. God has empowered you with a firm resolve that you must love yourself unconditionally; the good news is that the bad news about you isn't true. The best news is that the more you like yourself, the less concerned you will become with the opinions of others. The more you accept yourself for who you are, the more you make your decisions based on your purpose, goals, and values.

The people-skills pack I received from L.I.F.E. taught me how to be likeable and lovable, which resulted in me working toward a Godly attitude. At times, I felt lonely while transitioning and disconnecting from former relationships.

Evangelist Tracey Dawson extended a random act of kindness, unaware that I'd been hospitalized in Detroit, Michigan and was recuperating from a traumatic experience. After recovering at home for a short season, I returned to church.

She whispered, "I have something for you after the service."

When she gave me a beautiful journal, I fell on her shoulder and wept tears of joy. She hadn't known I'd been ill, but she had observed that I love to journal, so she felt led to give me this gift. God's message on the journal cover was timely. *"I am always with you, you have held My hand..."* *(Psalms 73:23)*

The healing virtue in unexpected blessings from unexpected places had an indelible, unforgettable, and tremendous impact. She deposited God's unconditional, no-strings-attached love, and I received God's love through His loving, observant, and obedient servant. He cares; He's able.

The ultimate purpose of love is to understand your belief systems, know who you are, and reinvent yourself. The most effective way to change is to reevaluate and activate a new system to love. Forgiveness is the final form of love.

The way to forgive becomes simple when you think of the other person. The Law of Substitution shows that the only way to replace one way of thinking is to replace it with another. Instead of thinking about how much someone has hurt you or affected your life in a negative way, replace it with a prayer similar to one like this: "God bless this person; I forgive this person for everything, and I wish this person well. I accept my responsibility for this conflict, and I substitute my hurt by taking it to the cross and nailing it there. It's not about me, but it's all about caring for this person and pleasing You, God. Amen."

It can be tempting to ignore others because they snub you, but you can't show them love by ignoring them. When you encounter difficult people who refuse to accept your forgiveness or gestures of love, the responsibility no longer lies on you.

When I am offended, I fall to the ground with my face in the carpet, arms and legs prostrate before God, and pray the prayer of forgiveness. Deliverance requires that I maintain the gain daily.

David Seamands teaches the principles for forgiveness. The first step is to let go of any desire for revenge. Many people fantasize about getting even. Even though most people would never follow through with those daydreams, it's vital not to even think about plotting revenge. Next, Seamands instructs the injured to release the person who did the hurting from responsibility for your pain.

Another important thing to do is to allow Jesus to carry your burdens for you. Ask yourself, "What does God want me to learn from this experience?" Usually, if you examine your own pain, you can quickly locate others around you who are also hurting. Take the energy you would have used on nursing the grudge and, instead, use it to minister to others. Ask God to give you strength to forgive and forget; don't neglect thanking God for allowing you to forgive. Lastly, don't bring up the episode and pain again. It is no longer yours; it now belongs to God.

My parents, Mr. and Mrs. O'Dell Nelson, Sr. Married for 61½ years until Dad's demise on February 10th, 2009. My mom was an excellent example of unconditional love; she gave dad a family, something he never had as a child.

A TIME TO REFLECT:

1. What makes you a lovable person?

   _____

   _____

   _____

   _____

2. What traits do you still need to work on?

   _____

   _____

   _____

   _____

3. What challenges do you need to overcome
   in order to accept God's love fully?

   _____

   _____

   _____

   _____

4. What crosses do you feel God is asking you
   to bear?

   _____

   _____

_____

_____

5. Whom do you need to forgive? What are
   some of the steps you need to take in order
   to forgive?

   _____

   _____

   _____

   _____

6. What do you need to do to prepare your
   heart so that you can honestly make this
   statement: "I resolve to change and fulfill
   The Law of Love and use my Master Key
   of Love to embrace my privilege to possess
   and maintain an intimate relationship with
   God"?

   _____

   _____

   _____

   _____

REPEAT THE RESOLUTION:

I resolve to change and fulfill The Law of Love and use my Master Key of Love to embrace my privilege to possess and maintain an intimate relationship with God.

CHAPTER 2

CHALLENGED TO LIVE THE ABUNDANT LIFE:
OBEDIENCE IS THE KEY

Living life requires that you teach others the love that you need to live by yourself. Life skills are essential to living an abundant life. Since Jesus is the shepherd and we Christians are His sheep, and since sheep are dumb, we follow Him in His example of obedience.

The pressures and problems of modern living are driving many people to search for meaning and purpose in life. There is a hunger and thirst for something more beyond the present state. Baby Boomers sacrificed and provided for their children and future generations to acquire more education, affluence, power, position, and success, but missed the true definition of abundance. Personally, I lacked the knowledge of true abundant living. An abundant life does not consist of the profusion of things.

Abundance is your birthright and you attract abundance to your life. Are you willing to accept the challenge to learn the true meaning of abundant living? You cannot afford to attract something that wasn't meant for you. Soul ties with the wrong people can alter your thinking and change your life.

If you don't feel secure in the unconditional love of God, it will be difficult to comprehend the promise of an abundant life.

Around five years ago, I purchased a stuffed rabbit that played "Jesus Loves Me" to use as an object lesson for the launching of our Women's Life Skills series, "Receiving God's Love." Listening to the words of the song is more reassuring today than the first day I rehearsed the song. Anna B. Warner wrote the powerful lyrics. "Jesus loves me, this I know, for the Bible tells me so. Little ones to Him belong, I am weak but He is strong." I sang this precious song until the words were ingrained in my brain. The toy rabbit may run on batteries, but God's love for us is everlasting. I still listen to that song today. Now, I have the love right, I have Christ right, and I have my life right.

The key is to live your life in Him. Acts 17:28 states, "For in Him we live, and move, and have our being."

Faith requires love to move in the progressive flow of the spirit of a living God. The risk-taking experiences transitioning from the world into the Church and learning how to live in the Kingdom of God provide characteristics and skills for victorious living. Your faith in God saves you; however, you may constantly be reminded that you live from faith to faith.

Many believers consciously know that they live for God, but unconsciously have a sense-of-entitlement mentality, which infects and affects attitudes, dispositions, and faith. Many people believe that salvation is a badge of distinction that shields them from the calamities that others experience. They believe that their journeys in life end with success but fail to realize that should not be the ultimate goal. Instead, significant living is

God's goal. What a rude awakening many will be in for if they don't change their perceptions and attitudes. Life and living is a balance of failure and success.

The Bible teaches that the moral fall of man began when sin entered the world. Mankind has been challenged or been attacked by the enemy to defy what God has promised. Ever since the thief came to steal, to kill, and to destroy the promise of abundance, humans tend to focus on negativity rather than the specific intent of God-centered living.

One system of theology that describes the most literal interpretation of the Bible is known as Dispensationalist. There is a period in the Bible that many call the Dispensation of Innocence, which refers to the time before Adam was born. God created man to live in perfect harmony with himself. During this time, there was no disease, evil, or imperfections. God created Adam and Eve in His image. Sin had not yet touched their lives. They had eternal souls, as well as free will. They walked hand in hand with God throughout the garden, developing an intimate relationship with their Creator. This period is the shortest of the seven dispensations.

When a void and darkness occurred on Earth, the heavens shifted. God restored His habitation by recreating His original provisions for man. The time after Adam shifts life into the Dispensation Of Conscience. After Adam and Eve disobeyed God, humans experienced the battle of the wills in living a conscious, intentional life for God. The Law of Cause and Effect by Isaac Newton, which states for every action there is an opposite and equal reaction, reflects the inner turmoil. Obedience is the key for momentum in God.

Mankind experienced a different life after Jesus came to give everyone the opportunity for an abundant life in Him. Some think that becoming a born-again Christian means there will no longer be pain or trials. The life of Jesus shows that an abundant life is not pain-free.

If you truly believe there is, or should be, a pain-free life, then you are being led down a deadly path full of frustration, disappointment, disillusion, and distrust. Soon, you will begin to think that each challenge you encounter is a curse rather than a blessing, which provides the opportunity to grow and become closer to Jesus.

If life were easy for anyone, it would make sense that Jesus should be the one who deserved an easy life. His culture and environment of His birth, however, was meager; His parentage and family life was unique; the attempts on His life were numerous; His choice to allow unfair attacks on His character speaks volumes; His unconditional love resulted in disloyalty and betrayal from friends; and His death on the cross is incredible.

Yet, He operated with the Law of Love on that old rugged cross. There, in the shadow of the cross, Jesus bore our sins and felt the same physical pain that we experience. Since forgiveness is the ultimate form of love, Jesus endured your pain because He loves you. When you acknowledge that Jesus forgave your sins, yet you still have difficulty forgiving others, you are unconsciously expecting to receive some form of a payoff. It's important to examine your heart in order to discover what benefits you are receiving by hanging on to your grudges against others. You may worry that if you let go of the pain by forgiving the person who hurt you, you'll feel a sense of abandonment. The loss of that relationship may suddenly feel more real and will be something you have to acknowledge. By maintaining this debilitating behavior, you can blame someone else for your character flaws.

Jesus encourages you to make the decision to forgive because He is the Way, the Truth, and the Life; without Him, there is no life. He is the role model for the humanity and divinity of men. He sacrificed His life to give you a better life. Jesus knew His purpose for life and living even before the foundation of the world.

The way to discover your pre-designed purpose is by experiencing pain and suffering. Your misery will soon become your testimony, and you'll want to go out into the world and minister to others. Your mess or mistakes become your message. Your tears turn into your triumphs. Your pain develops into your purpose. Victims make excellent victors. Search your life and find your purpose by sacrificing for others.

Years ago, I dreamed of moving to Youngstown, Ohio. I truly loved Bishop Norman L. Wagner. He had a great mystique about him that emanated Jesus in his own life. Yet, I felt safe and comfortable at home in Michigan.

My marital problems were resolved when my husband, Benny, left me for a younger woman. My daughter, La Shawn, and I moved into a new townhouse on Eastern Michigan University's student housing complex. God managed to heal all of my relationships that had been broken because of my marriage.

I could feel God's grace wash over me as He began the healing process. I experienced joy and peace. He even took away my fear of public speaking because He had big plans for me. I became one of seven female team members, known as "The Third Division." We preached our seven-minute trial sermons. Together, we developed skills as we met once a month. God stood up within me and helped me preach the first message, "What Is the Abundant Life?" My knees trembled, chills ran down my spine, and sweat poured off my face; yet still, God gave me the strength to deliver that message. During that first message, I explained that living an abundant life meant following the Shepherd. In St. John 10:10, Jesus states, "The thief cometh not, but for to steal, and to kill, and to destroy: I am come that they might have life, and that they might have it more abundantly." Jesus came to earth to help you live the best life possible. In order to have that wonderful, abundant life, you must follow Jesus during every step of your journey. If you do stray, Jesus, like a good shepherd, will search for you and bring you back into His fold.

I followed the Lord through the valley of divorce. During times of sickness, I stumbled after him on trembling legs. When loneliness threatened to overwhelm me, Jesus held my hand and reminded me I was not alone. When domestic violence became a part of my life, Jesus gave me the strength to escape. While others rejected me, Jesus enfolded me in His loving arms. Together, He helped me through the lean times and taught me countless lessons. During these valleys of my life, I realized that an abundant life required me to possess a servant's heart while living a life of service.

When you hear God calling you to go out and do something, you need to answer His calling, even if it is something that terrifies you. He will never leave nor forsake you. You can try to fight with Him, but in the end, He'll win because your arms are too short to box with God. The sooner you throw off your gloves, the better your life will become.

My first experience in ministering the message, "What is the Abundant Life?" exhilarated me. Eight years later, my third message, "Broken to Be Made Whole," became a book by the same name. Yes, Jesus had those plans laid out for me before I even realized it myself. Publishing the book helped me to minister to more of His children in ways I never anticipated when I first presented that message. When you feel comfortable, beware because it's possible God will have plans for a great transition and spiritual shift in your life. When God sends commands from Heaven's quarters, you must immediately step in obedience, follow Him, and move!

God issued an unexpected clarion call for me. A clarion call is a strong and clear request for a person to take a specific action. God told me to leave my extended family and move with my daughter to Youngstown, Ohio. The elite Calvary Christian Academy of Higher Learning offered me a position as a social studies and psychology teacher and counselor. Once we settled into our new home, we needed to find a new church family in the area. Mt. Calvary Pentecostal Church, *The Place Where Dreams Do Come True*, was the answer to my prayers.

My former church, Messiah's Temple, and my family gave us separate farewell parties before we left Ypsilanti, Michigan on September 4, 1983. As my friend, Carol Hollis, drove us across the state line, I read a sign: "WELCOME, OHIO LOVES YOU." Immediately, the Lord spoke. "You have just left your Egypt-land, filled with pain, tears, and suffering. You have entered your Canaan-land, which flows with milk and honey. You will be greatly blessed. It won't be easy; look not to the left nor the right, but look to me. You must defeat the enemies in Canaan Land before you possess all of your promises.

"Just as Abraham had to leave his support system in the land of Ur and move to a new land, a new beginning, likewise, your move is to bless both of you. I will bless those who bless you and curse those who curse you. You will be a great blessing to my people in ministry. You will receive abundant financial blessings. You will marry a good, loving companion. Your daughter will be blessed, and I will make up the difference for all of your sacrifices, and bless you for your obedience."

The offer of the teaching position, a divine setup, opened the door of a lifetime to be repositioned and mentored under the leadership of the late, Honorable Bishop Norman L. Wagner. His memory and labor of love left a legacy to challenge us to continue the work of God in excellence and become exceptional.

As I was learning how to serve God's people full-time, promise after promise manifested. Eight years later, Luther and I were married. God provided me with a wonderful husband just as He promised me. He also blessed us to be able to live debt-free after years of living frugally.

My first book, *Broken to Be Made Whole,* was an unexpected blessing to thousands. The late Yvonne Wagner, "Miss Tel-a-World," loved and promoted many books for years. She deemed me, "The Best-Selling Author," and showed me how to publish books in several languages.

My daughter was blessed to graduate from Youngstown State University debt-free, while we were transitioning from a single-parent family into a two-parent family. After La Shawn married David, we have seen an abundant increase to a Godly-blended family spanning five generations.

Yet, excellence in leadership seemingly eluded me. For thirty-eight years, I felt like the man at the pool of Bethesda, lying on the stairs waiting to be healed. I felt paralyzed because I was not moving forward as a leader.

As a Christian, for thirty-eight years, I asked the question, "What is the Abundant Life? Is it really a wonderful life filled with promises, dreams, and visions?"

Bishop Norman L. Wagner said, "Life is a gift from God, but living life is an art-form which requires life skills."

Life is a journey, filled with swift transitions from the womb to the tomb. Life is an absurd process of brokenness and wholeness that challenges and changes you. You make changes and choices that heal your broken soul and make you whole with God's help. Life is wholeness that is sacred and makes us holy. Life is *Loving Intensely,*

Forgiving Eternally. Forgiveness is love in excellence. Orrin Woodward stated, "L.I.F.E. is Living Intentionally for Excellence." Excellence allows us to live the life we always wanted to live.

John 14:6 says, "Jesus saith unto him, 'I am the way, the truth, and the life: no man cometh unto the Father, but by me.' " Suffragan Bishop C. Shawn Tyson stated, "Life is the absolute fullness of living, the essential and ethical, which belongs to God. Life is the union of the spirit of God with the spirit of man, after Jesus subjected Himself to the will of God, fulfilling the promise that the Lord will perfect those things concerning us."

The search for purpose and the search for significance is the ultimate fulfillment for our existence. Abundance is access to the intellect of God – the mind of Christ. The charisma of God is to empower us to think on a higher level of content and character because we can never change our behavior until we change our minds.

Many people are looking for life in the wrong places. It should not be based on performance, obtaining status, power, position, and wealth; but it is moving into a place and posture of prayer, allowing God to release witty inspiration, supernatural ideas, and economic independence. Many define significance by performance, but significance should be expressed by purpose.

Many live under the illusion of a Success Syndrome, which means working their way up the ladder. On the other hand, searching for significance, not success, allows you to let God control your life. Because our flesh is never satisfied, many people will desire more success and never be fully satisfied. If you humble yourself before the Lord, He will exalt you and provide for the vision. Cautious, unbridled ambition is a success principle; being calm and confident are traits of the Significance Principle.

God reveals that abundance requires developing life skills under certain conditions, which include unbelievable challenges; making difficult choices; painful changes; unexpected process-delayed promises; beautiful dreams or horrific nightmares; immature victims turning into mature victors; religious hypocrites transforming into powerful believers led by the Spirit of the living God. The indwelling Spirit of God is rest.

Abundant Life is now living on the plus side of life. God wants you to follow your heart's desire.

First, God releases you from living your life based on obligations of debt and grants you access into the life of God's priorities.

Second, you have access to the laws of mastery that entrust properties and funds, which steps you beyond mediocrity. God allows you to live within your harvest.

Third, you are given the inheritance of authority, confidence, supernatural peace, power, wisdom, favor, and an attitude of expectation of increase and hope.

Fourth, you possess the total manifestation of the entire aspects of a whole person in character, competence, commitment, choices, and change that reflects Jesus. What hurt or hindered you yesterday won't bother you today.

If you want to live an abundant life, take the time to rest and live a life of significance. Be obedient to God. As you slow down and live each moment, remember to make time to pray every day. Find ways to manage your stress. You can do this by deep breathing, exercising, or talking problems out with a trusted counselor.

Remember to forgive others just as Christ has forgiven you. Obey God's Word by faith and produce your victory by using your voice and say what you see. It's important to rejuvenate your mind and body by getting the proper amount of sleep. Try to take short naps during the day if you feel overtired. Choose to understand that the Holy Ghost is rest and comes to lead and guide you into God's truth, not to provide you with the American dream.

Instead of worrying and fretting over the situations in your life, use that energy to worship God with praise, singing, and prayer. Remember that humility is a virtue. Don't do things for individual praise; instead, do things in the name of

Jesus. Meditate day and night to obtain Godly success and the peace that passes all understanding.

Embrace solitude and silence daily. Meditation and journaling will help you express your emotions and align them with the right thoughts. The Bible gives excellent advice in Philippians 4:8. "Finally, brethren, whatsoever things are true, whatsoever things *are* honest, whatsoever things *are* just, whatsoever things *are* pure, whatsoever things *are* lovely, whatsoever things *are* of good report; if *there be* any virtue, and if *there be* any praise, think on these things." In other words, think as God thinks.

In Psalm 46:10, it states, "Be still, and know that I *am* God: I will be exalted among the heathen, I will be exalted in the earth." Each day and night, meditate on this verse. Listen to God when He points out subtle distractions. Shut your emotions down and shut your negative voice down. You are talking to yourself too much and, worse yet, listening to yourself. Too much busyness, too many distractions, and a lack of focus are non-productive.

You are gifted, highly favored, yet blinded by your hidden motive to heal vicariously by helping others. You have obeyed the Word in pursuit of an abundant life, and at the appointed time, you will live to see His goodness in the land of the living. Your labor is not in vain; just trust Him.

Our team mentor, Minister Aaron Thomason, encouraged us to stay focused on Jesus and the dreams we are looking for because they are within our grasp.

Weights and sins create a dysfunctional relationship that will lead you into crooked thinking, crooked places, and lack of focus. It is imperative to surround yourself with focused people.

"If we don't stay focused on the formula of God, the spirit of distraction will deceive us and the enemy's intent is to cause us to turn on the preachers and pastors as leaders in the house. When our heart condemns us we cannot preach." Dr. I.V. Hilliard

The right people will direct us to Jesus, who is the author and finisher of our faith. He will teach us how to pave the way for generations to come. Jesus, as a finisher, requires consistency and perseverance. He stayed focused on why He began the race in the first place, endured the cross, and disregarded the shame for the joy that was set before Him.

Jesus disregarded the fact that He helped and healed people but still wound up on the cross. The process set before us hurts, but it also says, "*I love you.*" Our Lord died without any guarantee that humanity would accept Him. You must stay focused and on course because the weight and the sin provide a purpose in the process. They are temporary places that you must move away from and shift to the ways and example of Jesus. You can never be comfortable with sin, yet it seems to be justified as acceptable in many churches. You have been endowed with power, authority, and the inner resolve to keep pressing on, even when you feel discouraged. Your delegated power of position as a witness empowers you to love others and provide them with the opportunity for an Abundant Life. Even though they may mock you, you can remain focused and carry your cross for the joy of others.

I began to hear the Shepherd's voice; hear the sounds; note the songs I sang from my heart. Is this my song or someone else's? I found my voice and sang. Live your own life (your God-given dream), not what others think you should be doing at this time. Abundant Life required obedience to fulfill God's dream for me to become an author. He uses His books for evangelism, healing, and legacy. Praying and writing develops dedication, devotion, direction, discernment of dead things in life, discipline, and divine revelation.

Life is a journey filled with many transitions.

A TIME TO REFLECT:

1. What does success mean to you?

    _____

    _____

    _____

    _____

    _____

2. What are some of the challenges you face
    today?

    _____

    _____

    _____

    _____

    _____

    _____

    _____

3. What do you think Jesus is trying to teach
    you through these challenges?

    _____

    _____

_____

_____

_____

4. In what areas of your life do you need to slow down and rest in Jesus?

_____

_____

_____

_____

_____

5. What are some of the negative lies you tell yourself each day?

_____

_____

_____

_____

_____

6. With what positive affirmations can you replace the lies?

_____

_____

_____

_____

_____

7. What type of countenance or attitude are
    you wearing?

_____

_____

_____

_____

_____

_____

_____

REPEAT THE RESOLUTION:

I resolve to live "An Abundant Life" through the
Rest Principle: to get plenty of peaceful, spiritual
rest in a chaotic world, and with a servant's heart
yielded to a life of obedience and service.

CHAPTER 3

CHALLENGED TO TAKE A STEP BEYOND:
WALK ON BY FAITH

After you decide to live the abundant life, you are ready to take another step beyond where you are now. The following is an excerpt from an article I wrote for our Pentecost in Perspective Leadership Conference: "Walk in the Light, the beautiful Light; God is light, and in Him, there is no darkness at all." I accept the challenge to be guided by vision, for where there is no sight of God, we perish from the lack of knowledge.

I was learning to flow in the momentum of God and move from stress to strength. When there are progressive movements forward, it is important to understand that psychological stress may interfere with spiritual progress. I was making deliberate steps, walking circumspectly before God.

When life's challenges cause things to change, such as blissful weddings, new jobs, babies, and unexpected events, those changes are stressful. Fear and uncertainties of life create stress. Some people experience spiritual emptiness, emotional burnout, and physical exhaustion, which take their toll on their lives; others respond with healthier, joyful behavior. It is important to develop skills of perception to master debilitating emotions during stressful transitions.

Have you ever been in a place in your life where you feel you've become oblivious to your surroundings? You feel like the walking dead. You seem to be stuck in a time zone between the kingdom of life and death. Does it appear that you are not making any progress? Are you still in the same condition, sick, once declared healed, but now sick again? You have been there for too many years! It's time to admit and identify personal strongholds.

A stronghold is any pretense that sets itself up against the knowledge of God: anything that becomes a bigger preoccupation in your mind than the truth and knowledge of God, anything that dwarfs His truth and knowledge in your imagination (See 2 Corinthians 10:4-5).

When I talk to friends too long on the telephone; counsel others all night; watch "Lifetime Movie Network;" Satan builds strongholds. God, with a small still voice said, "Turn the television off, and change your phone to an unlisted number."

I loved God enough to obey His voice, and by faith, to change my phone number immediately. It took me a little longer to turn the television off, but I finally disconnected my cable too.

God reestablishes boundaries when you fail to establish them and helps you eliminate toxic relationships. Familiarity breeds contempt. I believed if I continued doing what was familiar to me, I'd receive great blessings; that my shattered dreams and broken visions would miraculously come to fruition. I truly believed as a minister and counselor that I was serving God's people in love and was in the center of His Will.

Flawed thinking patterns created actions with conditional strings attached and strongholds that matured from molehills into mountains. I was in a crisis of faith.

Your life experiences can ensnare you and may seem to immobilize you in your health, your finances, your spirit, your relationships, and God's ministries. You have spent endless, countless hours, months, and years in time, stuck somewhere, going nowhere, thinking you have arrived. Your wheels are stuck in the mud without any traction or momentum, and you haven't gone anywhere yet.

Frustrations occur when you don't understand God's timing. You settled in a place that God intended to be a process, a temporary, transitory place. Once there, you placed a period, thinking the story was finished. You became mediocre, stuck, trapped, and stagnant. You may have feared that your dreams would never come to pass. Are you willing to take a step beyond and replace the period with a comma? God is the author and finisher of your faith, not you.

St. John 5:6 states, "Now a certain man was there who had an infirmity thirty-eight years. When

Jesus saw him lying there, and knew that he already had been in that condition a long time, He asked him, 'Do you want to be made well?' " Some would automatically think the man would definitely want Jesus to heal him. Sometimes, though, people become content with the familiar, even if the familiar is full of pain. Remember, love is action. Jesus had a plan of action for this man.

1. Identify the presenting problem: The man was stuck in a generational curse.

2. Provide the truth: Jesus offered to meet him at the point of his physical and emotional needs.

3. Equip him to arise: Literally, Jesus healed him, allowing him to stand up and be free from disease.

4. Redeem: The man had to change his mindset in order to realize his life would be different because of Jesus.

This man is an object lesson for many people because he responded with excuses and complaints; He didn't want to leave his comfort zone and wondered what he would do if Jesus healed him.

He'd only known sickness and handouts. Psalm 37:23 states, "The steps of a good man are ordered by the Lord." Get up. Arise. Move in the momentum of God, not in your own pace. Change! Move from fear to faith to go forward in God.

No one wants to admit when she is wounded, hurt, and scared. While some emotions may be embarrassing, they are important indicators that your thoughts and feelings are out of alignment. Something happens to some people that delays their development on their journeys to their destinies. Whatever brokenness you experience, it can actually be a catalyst for transformation and maturity.

The abuse or misuse of people was the passionate inspiration fostering the inception of "Restoration Ministries" and "Quality of Life Ministries of Inner Healing." God illuminated the need for inner healing in the churches, and equipped me with the sensitivity and compassion to discover and fulfill my God-given purpose of helping others.

God's grace allows entrance into His heart, and His heart into mine. What a friend we have in Jesus. Apostle Paul states in 2 Corinthians 1:3-4, "Blessed be God, even the Father of our Lord Jesus Christ, the Father of mercies, and the God of all comfort; Who comforteth us in all our tribulation, that we may be able to comfort them which are in any trouble, by the comfort wherewith we ourselves are comforted of God."

Within a church family, the need for counseling will always exist. The complexity of life and living often places one in a maze with no exit sign to normality. It is at this point one seeks the advice of many and sometimes the counsel and the insight of God.

Though the counsel is based upon the teaching of Scriptures, you must understand that the maze is constructed by the ways of erring men; consequently, one must understand the maze and the fallen man, as well as the teachings of Jesus.

Emotions can move you away from God. Most emotions become your most formidable enemy.

Ninety percent of people are emotional and struggle with negativity. Instead of dealing with their emotions, many people choose to react to them in anger or other harmful ways. Our Adamic nature of the flesh chooses to focus on the negatives in life and ignores the positives.

Observe your choices, attitude, and behavior while shifting from God-centered, image-bearing living to self-centered living. The meaner or more frightened person indicates his or her choice of movement to self-occupation and self-pity. The immature person chooses childish and inappropriate reactions. She is merely acting out her pain in her relationships. There is a need for qualified, Christian counselors to lead people through transitory places in life's journey.

Clinical depression and anxiety neurosis were just two of several diagnoses and darkness I learned to live through. Depression has several definitions, but my specific intention is to identify depression as *a thief who stole my gifts, attempted murder, and almost destroyed my life.*

Depression is often a byproduct of worrying about what other people think of you. Breaches in relationships cause wounds or gaping holes, resulting in repressed anger.

It is a lie when parents try to console children with the famous cliché, "Sticks and stones may break my bones, but words will never hurt me." I allowed words to almost destroy me.

It was important for me to relearn how to think, and to think of myself as God sees me, and not react to other people's thoughts. My soul (thoughts, emotions, decisions) had to be anchored in the Lord. Vocational Rehabilitation, in Ann Arbor, Michigan closed my case after two years of intensive counseling and networking to provide community mental health resources.

According to research conducted by the National Institute of Mental Health, anxiety disorders are the number one mental health problem in the United States. Nearly forty million people have suffered from panic attacks, phobias, or other anxiety disorders in the past year. From the 1990s to the beginning of the 21st century, panic and anxiety reached epidemic proportions.

Anxiety is prevalent because it is an outcome of cumulative stress acting over time with physiological and emotional dynamics. Stress is at an all-time high, in and out of the church, because the culture has changed over the last thirty years to an increased rate of technology that deprived us of adequate time to adjust to the transitions.

Secondly, lack of a consistent, sacred set of standards and values traditionally prescribed by the church leaves a vacuum in which people are left to fend for themselves and create their own moral standards. Some of our youth are more aggressive in their behavior and face social challenges in their experiences while transforming from natural to spiritual living. The world offers more opportunities and motivates personal ambition as subtle distractions. Today, ambition must be managed; otherwise, the saying, "Doing whatever my hands find to do," may pull and tear you in too many directions.

God is issuing a clarion call. It is a universal call to everyone. He is searching for believers who will respond in the spirit to move into a new season of Abundant Life and Exceptional Living. The complexity of human living is often created by the missed step, tripping between faith and trust. In the meantime, the gap between the imposter and the real me is a bridge of obscurity. Hidden in obscurity is the unknown process, which includes the changing challenges of culture, perceptions, customs, personalities, parentages, values, and experiences.

In God's time, you will learn to walk through transitions. Transition is the passage from one stage of life to another place, requiring movements in a timely process from a natural location to a spiritual location in God. You no longer walk in the same steps, known as your mode of operation. Others could always depend on your predictable behaviors and habits.

I left that place seven steps ago with a vision and am now taking seven new steps forward. This year is the release from the seven steps of lean years in my soul, lying around in immaturity and stepping into the spiritual release. I'm walking in the next seven steps of the prophetic plan of Jesus to be healed, restored, and made whole. The weather is better standing on my feet.

Transformation is the awareness of something within that is hindering your maturity and identifying your blind spots. My disability included painful, embarrassing challenges, but I answered the call to come up higher. The dream remained in my spirit in spite of the emotional struggle and tug-of-war. It was painful.

Pain has a purpose in the process; even though you experience tests, temptations, and pitfalls, pain is a motivator for change. Once you've been in a crisis, it becomes easier to let go of ways that don't work anymore. Instead, you will cling to God's way. Shift; don't live in automatic, but shift, learn new standards, new principles, and how to change gears. Pain is inevitable, but misery is optional.

Take your misery and use it to help others. You must live through the pain to develop the power. Turn rejection into energy and creativity.

If you don't rise, you'll die, and others around you will die spiritually. You are that significant to God. Have confidence in God, and confidence in others. Eventually, you will develop confidence in knowing that you can do all things through Christ who gives you strength. Every idol, whether it is your spouse, your children, money, your job, ambition, or television, must be dethroned from God's throne and cast out.

Before your dreams manifest, you must become determined, persistent, and patient while God is changing your character and attitude. The proof that you trust God and His Word is evidenced when God is testing and trying your faith.

You have the faith to step out on God's promise; however, the enemy will challenge you with adversity, and you may trip. When that happens, you'll be tempted to go backward rather than forward.

You cannot see your future, the past is too dark, and the present lacks focus and feels obscure. The faith you used to get to your destination depleted your energy. Then, you begin to second-guess yourself, but remember that destiny is beyond you.

You have no choice but to take the next step. When you walk in these steps, you will discover what God has planned for your life. First, you must heal yourself emotionally, stand back on your feet and continue your journey to living an abundant life.

When Jesus ministered to the man who had the infirmity for thirty-eight years, the man wanted to dip in the water, but Jesus offered him the Living Water. Then, He cast down strongholds (half-truths) that had been protecting the man's ego from pain.

Once you uproot the embedded lie, Jesus will deposit the truth into your heart, and the spirit of defilement will no longer have a body to dwell in or to incarcerate you. You'll be free from the bondages of depression, anxiety, embarrassment, anger, resentment, rejection, and abandonment. Healing requires the discipline to cast out negative habits, thoughts, and feelings, and the discipline to learn new information that replaces the lies and distorted perceptions.

Just make the transition from the bed and stand up. Have faith in God. Arise, get up, and don't go back to that place anymore. The man in the parable was able to find the strength to trust and obey Jesus. In doing so, Jesus freed him from his crippled and useless body. Next, Jesus looked him in the eyes and commanded, "Sin no more."

Not all illness is caused by sin, though, so it's vital for you to recognize negative thoughts and feelings that may be crippling you. Realize that feelings aren't necessarily facts. You may be telling yourself lies. "I'm not worthy of forgiveness. No one loves me. I deserve to have bad things happen to me." In order to live the abundant life that Jesus has given you, you need to stop believing those lies, and instead, focus on God's promise. Isaiah 60:1-5 reads, "Arise, shine; for your light has come...

because the abundance of the sea shall be turned to you. The wealth of the Gentiles shall come to you."

At 4:00 p.m. on Sunday, January 12, 2014, at New Bethel Church, Calvary Ministries, the voice of God thundered through First Lady, Evangelist Krista M. Tyson, as she hand-delivered a Heaven Union Telegraph from Isaiah 43 and Psalm 66:12 entitled, "The Rite of Passage" to her audience. She deposited love and light as she focused on bridging the gaps during our transitions of life.

She stated, "Decisions in temporary places affect destiny when living in the permissive will rather than the divine will of God." To make transitions is a chance to get your life back on track; get your thinking right; get your reputation back; get your priorities in the correct order; right your previous wrongs; and make a change.

God allows these moments in order to help you correct your wrong-doings; He wants to change your heart and mind so that you may move beyond the ruts in your life. This allows you to move from your past into God's presence. God continues to push you in order to move you onward.

In the Garden, Jesus realizes what is coming next and cries out to the Father. "And he went a little farther, and fell on his face, and prayed, saying, 'O my Father, if it be possible, let this cup pass from me: nevertheless not as I will, but as thou wilt.' " (Matthew 26:39) Even though Jesus felt the turmoil, He knew that God's Will must be followed. Inside the cup are bitterness, pain, poison, chastisement, loneliness, disobedience, guilt, depression, anger, and beatings.

These sufferings were never meant to hurt you or make you turn your back on God. These trials are to give you a greater understanding of God; allowing you to experience suffering so He can set you on the right path. Your confession will follow you forever and allow you to move forward.

Walking in the natural way requires progress made by controlled falling. When you walk, you push yourself off balance with one leg and foot. If the next step is placed in the correct spot to support your body then you won't fall. Likewise, deliberate actions in life allow you to maintain the proper balance in today's world.

The Bible shows how God holds His hand out to you when you take a spiritual misstep and find your actions caused you to come crashing down. "The steps of a good man are ordered by the Lord: and he delighteth in his way. Though he fall, he shall not be utterly cast down: for the Lord upholdeth him with his hand." (Psalm 37:23-24) God promises to help you up, and He will nurse you back to good spiritual health once more.

The spiritual definition of walking in the light is to live with wisdom, truth, purpose, vision, and righteousness as opposed to walking or living in moral or spiritual error, evil works, or ignorance.

Light is a synonym for truth. I had been searching for the Guiding Light to illuminate my experiences of prolonged, psychosomatic illnesses that became debilitating and resulted in an unhealthy gait; I didn't have swagger when I walked, no posture at all–I'd just lie around. After my transition, I began walking, stepping, skipping, dancing, and rejoicing. Now, the accusations and judgments that attack my faith in God are like darts that the devil throws to attempt to stop my gait with God.

MINSTRY IN PECULIAR PLACES

Timing is everything. March 23, 1983 will always be a monumental day in the lives of four of us who traveled to our Northern District Council from Ypsilanti, Michigan to Mt. Clemons, Michigan. The Missionary President began singing a melody of Blood Songs instead of presenting the preacher. We were perplexed because we expected to hear the Word of God before we left to attend a funeral.

While we were riding to the funeral, we laughed, chatted, and visualized our future as ministers, when suddenly, we felt a booming sensation as an eighteen-wheeler crushed the entire back of the car. The shattered windows caused the glass to fly everywhere. Shocked, stunned, and dazed, we turned to see a truck driver running toward the car to help us.

While waiting for the police, we began to witness to him about Jesus. I asked, "Do you know my Savior, Jesus Christ?"

Shaking his head, he answered, "No, I don't know Him, but I think that I just saw Him; you girls are supposed to be dead. I came within inches of rolling right over the car and crushing all four of you."

My friend, Nancy, who was driving the car and spotted the inevitable, heard God speak to her. "Keep driving; don't stop."

Her obedience to God saved our lives. God miraculously unlocked the car from the bottom of the truck. We were God's witnesses, and the accident turned a gloomy day into a wonderful opportunity to share God's love with a stranger. God placed us in His hand, covered us by His blood, protected us by His love, and allowed us to take a hit in order to glorify His name. As young ministers, we were oblivious to the circumstances, conditions, and damage to any material possessions, but we were on a specific assignment that day. We were destined to glorify God and serve others by depositing love and light. We are the salt of the earth and the light of the world. Perfect passion for Christ is the faith that saves lives.

Thirty-one years later, my husband and I traveled to Ypsilanti, Michigan to partake in fellowship and pray before continuing on to Detroit to spend time with my family. I hadn't been feeling well but didn't want to worry my family, so I went to see Evangelist Ivy Caddell at her day spa and told her I needed a massage. She anointed my body with holy oil. We stayed at another friend's house that evening where Evangelist Katrina Mitchell prepared a nutritious meal for us. In the evening, we all gathered to talk, pray and sing. Before Luther and I departed for Detroit, Katrina gave me a dress because my medication and my digestive system bloated my abdomen and my clothes were too tight and uncomfortable. I hardly had time to settle in and visit with my mother when I became dizzy and eventually blacked out. When I woke up, I was in Detroit-Sinai Grace Hospital's emergency room. I had been taking the wrong doses of the wrong medication. The increased intake of the prescription drugs caused an adverse reaction that could have resulted in death. These medications had a divine purpose, however; God showed me the truth. I could have become so dependent on the prescription drugs that it could have bordered on a serious addiction. After lying unconscious for two hours, I felt a spiritual presence smash into my chest. The pain caused me to sit straight up in bed. As I looked for the person who had hit me, I discovered no one was anywhere near me. Approximately ten emergency room staff rushed in and embraced me with the greatest care and concern while the two kind paramedics remained by my side to comfort me. The bright lights blinded me. The doctors admitted me, and I stayed in the hospital for three days.

On the third day, the same person who hit me in my chest, dressed in white, walked into the room and went directly to my roommate. Curious, I longed to follow her. I hesitated for a second because we were in the Fall Unit and protected by padded beds, our movement restricted, and warned not to make sudden moves without help. Therefore, I remained befuddled by her presence. I believe that I saw an angel unaware. The following day, my roommate continued to moan, groan, and call on Jesus.

Suddenly, I heard God speak, "This is your assignment; pray for her healing."

My husband and I held hands and prayed. "Dear Jesus, we ask that You watch over my roommate. Give her the strength to fight the pain. We ask that You totally heal her and allow her to rest in Your arms. Wash her in Your precious name and deliver her from the Evil One. In Jesus' name, we pray. Amen."

On March 23rd, shortly after we prayed, the doctor came in and discharged me. This pivotal moment in my destiny felt surreal. I was in a daze for days; it felt as though a dense fog covered my mind.

As soon as we returned home to Youngstown, I received a frantic call informing me that my friend, Jewell, was being flown to the University of Michigan Hospital because a brain aneurysm had ruptured, causing severe damage. The doctors told her family that her chances of surviving were slim. We immediately jumped in the car and headed back to the hospital to join her family and friends in a prayer vigil.

I turned to the wall and prayed, "God, we need a break. We can't handle this; please don't take Jewell–heal her." During the ten-hour surgery, God directed the doctors' hands. Hours earlier, they had virtually no hope for her recovery. She surprised the surgeons and lived as a miracle for months.

On the way home, my friend, Jacquie, texted me. I could hardly believe my eyes when I read her message. *I'm being admitted to St. Joe's Hospital in Warren, Ohio. The doctor said something is wrong with my heart.* While visiting her, we experienced *déjà vu* as we joined Jacquie and Levon in prayer for her roommate. We left rejoicing, and the doctor discharged Jacquie within two hours. We are prayer partners, and we have discovered that we often experience similar events.

Once again, God revealed the answer through the preaching of our pastor. Christians are intercessory prayer warriors and experience afflictions; however, Psalm 34:19 enlightens us. "Many are the afflictions of the righteous: but the Lord delivereth him out of them all." As you intercede for others, God works on your behalf, and your testimony will be, "It was good for me to be afflicted so that I learned of God's plans for me."

The love of God was illuminated that March 23rd, and it will always remind me of His greatness. God remained with me throughout the entire ordeal. I have been delivered from the fear of death, and I have been healed by the shadow of death. You never have to fear what you face by faith.

This supernatural healing has totally changed my walk with God, my faith in God, and my priorities to value people over possessions; to walk by faith, depositing love and light into the lives of others each day. I will never, ever be the same.

In retrospect, the Lord used a fellow sister in the Lord, Tosha Franklin, to declare life over me. While my hairstylist, Kim Laney, was preparing me for the trip, Tosha read long passages of meditations and scriptures pertaining to life over death. God had Kim make sure my appointment with her was at the right time. If we hadn't listened to God's voice and arrived earlier, there may have been a different outcome.

Prayer is vital to the process. Luther and I listened to these lessons and others to walk in our transitions as paraphrased by Pastor Dwight Dumas's Acrostic for Transition used during our five AM Ministry of Prayer and Intercession.

Timing–We thank you for showing us that perfect *timing* is crucial in knowing your season.

Revelation–We thank you, Lord, for *revealing* new solutions for old problems.

Attitude–We thank you, God, for the desire to carry our cross with a good *attitude*. We terminated our bad *attitude* and moved to destiny.

Negativity–We thank you, God for the ability to speak life into *negativity,* and now, the only negative reports we receive are from the doctors informing us that our biopsies are negative. We have learned to step into a positive mindset.

Steadfast–We thank you, God for your *steadfast* love, and for stamina, strength, and stability. We desire to see salvation for those who are in a difficult situation.

Ideas–We thank you, Lord, for giving us witty inventions and fresh *ideas.* We thank you for written books and successful businesses as they come to fruition.

Truth–We thank you, Lord, for your word that states, we shall know the *truth* and the truth shall set us free. Take away deception and transition us into speaking the truth everywhere we go.

Intimidation–We thank you, Lord, for the strength to transition into power and step out on faith to our release and for *intimidating* our enemies. Help us to bear fruit and fruitfulness in great abundance.

Opposition–We thank you, God, for making us stronger and powerful to come against the *opposition*. We have victory because no weapon formed against us can prosper.

New–We thank you because Revelation 21:5 reads, "Behold I make all things *new*."

Transitions require crossing bridges and walking down the pathways of life.

A TIME TO REFLECT:

1. What life changes are you experiencing right now?

   _____

   _____

   _____

   _____

   _____

2. How do you respond to the stressors in your life?

   _____

   _____

   _____

   _____

   _____

3. What changes do you need to make to your life to walk in transition?

   _____

   _____

   _____

_____

_____

4. What idols are you clinging to, and what
   steps can you take to focus more fully on
   Jesus?

   _____

   _____

   _____

   _____

   _____

5. God performs miracles every day; some
   people consider these coincidences, but
   those with a firm relationship with God
   know better. Where have you seen God's
   hand at work in your life in the last thirty
   days?

   _____

   _____

   _____

   _____

   _____

   _____

REPEAT THE RESOULUTION:

I resolve to change and live in the Law of Transition: Get up, get over it and keep moving by faith.

CHAPTER 4

CHALLENGED TO IMAGINE:
DREAMS OR NIGHTMARES

When you are living in a nightmare, it is impossible to dream the dreams of God. Dreams require the thoughts, mindset, and intellect to think like God. This life skill is also referred to as critical thinking.

As a Christian, you walk by faith and not by sight. Yet, the world has programmed you to worry. During your time of deprograming and rebooting your mind, you will discover how to wait, imagine, visualize, and regain your spiritual sight. The Bible provides numerous examples of dreamers and visionaries who have the capacity to foretell or predict their realities. Your conscious and subconscious mind is created to imagine, dream, and to visualize yourself performing and doing works for God. Proverbs 23:7 states, "As a man thinketh in his heart so is he." Are you ready to accept the challenge to develop Godly thinking and intellect?

You need quality time to develop your mind. Vince Poscente, a motivational speaker, quantifies the difference between the capacities of the conscious and the subconscious mind. In the course of thinking for just one second, the conscious brain stimulates two thousand neurons and the subconscious brain stimulates four billion neurons. Images formed in your subconscious mind have an overwhelmingly greater influence in shaping the vision by faith. The subconscious mind is the prime mover by a factor of two million to one. Internal conflict occurs between the will and imagination, much like the conflict the Apostle Paul experienced in Romans 7:15. "I do not understand what I do. For what I want to do, I do not, but what I hate I do." (New International Version)

When you program the conscious and the subconscious with faith and confidence, you experience a continual transformation in your mind. It requires work and discipline to acquire creativity, a great stress buster. If you want to be effective for God and with others in relationships, you need time for recovery while pressing through chronic stress and illness. You need to take time to dream again.

Dreams require a passionate pursuit of your purpose by seeing, imagining, picturing, and believing with all of your heart. Faith moves God to fulfill the dreams that He deposited in your heart. After all, it was His thought and His idea in the first place. God created you to think like Him.

Pure hearts, clean minds, and a hunger and thirst after righteousness is essential in maintaining and sustaining God's dream for you. Between the time God speaks the promise and the manifestation of the promise, the soul, as the transmitter, transmits the message to the spirit; the promise becomes ingrained within you until the promise becomes reality.

God's Dream, Human Struggle, Divine Victory

Unrelenting faith is necessary to maintain clarity and to focus on the results or the big picture. Faith is taking God's Word and acting on it no matter how long it takes. You will get weary and struggle while waiting, and that's when God sends glimpses of newsflashes from Heaven to your mind as encouragement to move in His momentum.

After recuperating from a nervous breakdown over thirty years ago, God ministered to me from the Creation Story, which left an indelible impact in my spirit. I meditate on it often to regain my grounding in living in the spiritual realm and release me from gravity that pulls me backwards.

While reading a beautiful poem by my friend, Sherry Wynne, I imagined a scenario of perfect life. I've included snippets of the poem in the following paragraphs. Dreams require faith and imagination. I can finally imagine myself in the original predesigned life script written for me. Please focus on the specific intent of a Godly image, which requires faith, imagination and the ability to dream.

"We were created in the mind of God as spiritual, soulful, and physical beings formed in glory. As God stepped into our voided places that He had set aside for mankind, glory filled emptiness, spirit moved, God spoke, and then the light shined. Light separated from darkness, waters from waters, and dry land from seas. And the earth brought forth grass, herbs of all kinds and fruit-yielding trees."

With Heaven and Earth finished, God began to work on His most ambitious plan. God provided a beautiful planet for mankind. He was concerned with all of our needs. When he made the first man, Adam, He realized that he would need a helpmate, so God created Eve from one of Adam's ribs.

God deeply loved Adam and Eve, but since He made them humans with free will, it wasn't long before they messed up. In giving them free will, God made Adam responsible for being morally and spiritually developed. God enjoyed talking and walking with Adam and Eve on a regular basis. Then one day, the serpent came along. He was a greedy and jealous creature. He devised a plan to force God's hand. By tricking Eve to eat from the Tree of Knowledge, and then encouraging her to have Adam eat the fruit as well, he guaranteed their destiny.

LIVING IN THE HOUSE THAT GOD BUILT

Before we were born, God predesigned us from His pattern of love. He wrote life scripts for each one of us. Then, He proceeded to create us from His thoughts and His imagination for His glory. Our sole purpose in life is to serve God's people in love, depositing love and light in order to glorify God.

God literally designed you so that you would dream the dreams of God, receive His promises, and never lack anything. The Law of Original Intent states that God predestined you to be you, before the foundation of the universe was formed. He thrust you into living in the original intentions of God, the spiritual realm, before you were born.

When I imagine myself as a whole creature, I think of being totally free to be the authentic, original me. You spend your entire life building the house of your personal faith, obedience, love, morality, and understanding–a house in which you can seek shelter in peace. In Genesis 1:26–31, God's goals for mankind were clear. Born with the intellect of God, Adam learned how to move by the speed of thought and dominate the works of creation.

TRICHOTOMY OR THREEFOLD COMPOSITION OF MAN

Body is the fleshly physical house that is *world conscious.* The body is the temple of the spirit and soul.

Soul is the emotional house that is *self-conscious.* The soul is the temple of the mind, emotions, and will.

Spirit is the spiritual house that is *God-conscious.* The spirit is the temple of The Holy

Spirit where the heart relates to God in prayer, praise, worship, and truth.

Man was born with a divine purpose, safe and secure, and had a sense of belonging. The body with its complex systems heals itself when the body, the mind, and spirit work as a team.

Adam and Eve were a team. Eve, mother of all life, was a beautiful *Ishahah* (woman). She defined the female role as the heart of the home, an emotional complement, super-qualified to provide love, nurturing, sensitivity, and warmth. We are beautiful *Ishahahs.* A significant delay occurred between the time God said He would make a "helper" for Adam and the time He actually made Eve. She was touched by God when taken out of the side of Adam and was the last of God's creation, His crowning glory. She was without blemish. She was learning a high sense of significance and Godly-esteem.

Adam, a handsome *Ish* (man), observed his roles as the priest, provider, protector of his home, and a friend of God as he minded the things of God.

He was totally God-centered. He presented himself before God daily and mastered knowing the voice of God.

However, when God took Adam's rib out of his side and made Eve, Adam was asleep. Sometimes, men are asleep while women are aware of God's Hand. Men, you are handsome *Ishes*.

GOD'S ORIGINAL INTENTIONS

Just as parents download their genetic code to us, God downloaded His divine DNA to Adam and Eve. He commanded them to multiply and reproduce spiritual seeds that would bring forth generations and generations after their own kind, spiritual connectors without any sin.

When God said, "Let us make man in our image," it signifies His sovereignty and majesty because traditionally, kings used the plural form in speaking of themselves. His image reflects His sinless, eternal, loving, and wise characteristics in our hearts. Every thought has a seed of positive fruit, which inherited the ability to think thoughts and speak seeds into good ground.

God's responsibility was to teach laws of cause and effect and their consequences. Man's responsibility was to obey and complete his God-given assignments, which resulted in Adam and Eve discovering who they really were and developing morals as they tilled the garden and connected with one another.

Adam and Eve were to develop the windows of opportunity for generations. All families have rules, attitudes, and patterns they learned while growing up. Governed by the law of homeostatic balance, the closer families observed the balance and enjoyed healthier family functions. God designed families to attach, bond, interrelate, and be interdependent on one another. Families were laboratories to prepare children for an abundant life.

Your security is in God. He will guide you back to your past when He deems it necessary. God gives you the ability to dream and imagine as He does, thinking and speaking your way into a better future. Everyone has problems and circumstances in life that they must navigate. You need to rise to the occasion. If you can dream it, with God's help, you can achieve it. When you know and understand your heart's desire, then you can see yourself as you really are. Think and plan strategically by keeping a scoreboard and measuring your successes. Don't let your background put your back on the ground. Picture yourself rising in Jesus' name. Feel secure in His arms.

SECURE ATTACHMENT PATTERNS

Recently, I took a class in Psychology of Intimate Relations at Youngstown State University. I learned about the importance of attachment styles and relationship dynamics.

Secure people don't feel the pressure to perform to earn their self-worth. They are able to express thoughts and opinions more confidently. They're not worried that they'll be harmed or bruised emotionally if others disapprove. They are not afraid of healthy anger, but view it as hope for change. Conflicts lead to vibrant and thriving relationships.

Secure people are more tolerant of others' mistakes because they don't see mistakes as signs of dishonesty or rejection. Anger is a catalyst that leads to forgiveness and restoration. Sensitive parents help children discover the solution; they don't solve the problem for them. They use negative feelings as an opportunity to build a bridge of intimacy and to deepen connections.

Secure people realize there's safety in other people, and they manifest a sense of trust and look to others for help when needed. When they experience losses, they don't feel like victims, even when they are. They engage in active problem solving and keep trying until they find meaning in pain.

Courage is to act in the face of fear when you determine that action is needed to gain confidence in God's ultimate purpose. Designed by the original intentions of God, you secure your identity in Him, develop and sustain Godly value systems, and healthy core belief systems. Courage also guarantees healthy choices.

CORE VALUES

To develop a secure attachment-relationship dynamic, your value system must be based on God's original intent. Choose:

1. love over hate
2. eternity over brevity of life
3. altruism over selfishness
4. personal hurt over revenge
5. honesty over lies
6. significance over failure
7. faith over fear
8. faithfulness over infidelity
9. social relationships over private interest
10. kindness over rudeness

THE IDENTITY THIEF

An important principle in the journey and process into great health, wholeness, and growth are boundaries. Violation of boundaries creates chaos. When violations occur in the Kingdom of God, the violent take the Kingdom by force. *I want my stuff back!*

When Adam violated God's boundaries, he was seduced into another world, unaware and in an unfamiliar place. The serpent developed a demonic system to try to make the Kingdom of God subservient to him.

Today, the struggle is that if the thief cannot defeat you by deceiving your mind, he will then try to destroy your body. Satan attacks God's Word in an attempt to prevent you from knowing God's Will.

God accomplishes His will on earth through truth; Satan accomplishes his purposes through lies.

The serpent tricked Eve into listening to him. He tempted her with the forbidden fruit. Lucifer knew that if Eve violated God's law, she would be destined to die, but because he was so hateful, he didn't care what would happen to Eve. When God confronted his precious humans, Adam blamed Eve while Eve blamed the serpent. God could no longer trust them in the paradise He created especially for them. After Eve realized she had disobeyed God, she didn't go to Satan for comfort. Instead, God saw them running away. As they stood before Him, they trembled in their shame. God killed an animal that shed blood, atoning for their sins. The serpent couldn't provide her any answers or comfort; only God had that power. He took the animal skin and made them clothing. This is important because it sets up the need for blood to be spilled in order to pay for their sins. This made it necessary for Jesus to come to earth and sacrifice His blood so that you might live forever with Him in Heaven. God expelled Adam and Eve out of the Garden of Eden. Next, God turned to the serpent and cursed him.

Adam and Eve were able to flee from the presence of Satan. Flight or fight is a physical reaction to avoid confrontation, which are responses for life-threatening situations. The body's red alert system prepares to take action and avoids potential danger or death.

WHY WE REACT THE WAY WE DO

This scenario captured the essence of The Law of Cause and Effect. Why do you act the way you do? Why do the innocent die, get hurt, abandoned, and neglected? Human beings act carelessly, cruelly, and maliciously toward each other. Bad things happen as a violation of God's law and consequences of sin and the environment.

Men become poor, unstable, and ill because of their environment. As people, we have a tendency to blame the negative conditions of our lives– illness, death, poverty and other ills–on God and perhaps others.

But the blame never belongs to God. Many times, we can be victims of another's sins. God anticipated the wretchedness of people and knew they'd worship other gods, material possessions, power, position, and popularity rather than the God of sacredness.

Once you accept Jesus as your personal Savior, you may wonder why you still struggle from time to time. Jesus atones for your sins, but He does not promise you a stress-free life. He does promise in Philippians 4:13 that through Christ, you can accomplish all things. Some people take this verse to mean if you ask Jesus for something, He will give it to you, or God will never give you more than you can handle. What the verse actually says is you need Christ in order to handle and overcome the difficulties of life. He never promises an easy road; just that He will always be by your side. Just like Adam and Eve experienced great difficulty sustaining a spiritual life and developing morality, likewise, today, Christians sometimes have challenges transitioning from the world and secular living into a sacred, holy lifestyle; but you must elevate your mind to perceive the higher purpose in suffering.

By understanding that evil is evil and good is good, you'll be able to maintain the moral and spiritual fiber of your core being. If you allow Him, God will take a bad situation and bring you out of it into an even better place than you can imagine.

Even in the midst of chaotic darkness, God is always good and present.

To think that you are exempt from the challenges of this life because you are a Christian is immature thinking. When you mature, you become receptive and are obedient to choose to believe the end results will work for your good. Romans 8:28 speaks of these matters. "And we know that all things work together for good to them that love God, to them who are the called according to his purpose."

After the fall of man in the Garden of Eden, the mirror cracked, and parents were no longer able to accurately reflect the true nature of God to their children. As a result, there were no perfect parents anywhere.

Since the days of Adam and Eve, every family has been dysfunctional in one way or another. Psalm 51:5 states, "Behold, I was brought forth in iniquity, and in sin my mother conceived me." Sin fractures the relationship between God and us and between others and us. It also creates a painful emotional distance and destroys the close fellowship God intended for us to enjoy.

In Genesis 3:7, we see what happened to Adam and Eve after disobeying God. "Then the eyes of both of them opened, and they knew they were naked; and they sewed fig leaves together for coverings." Today, you wear a different kind of F.I.G. (fear, insecurity and guilt) leaves, which introduce the defense mechanisms hidden in the subconscious mind to protect your ego and distorted image.

There are many different mental mechanisms people use to attempt to cover up depression or anxiety and to try to solve emotional problems.

1. Compensation – People may tend to overachieve in one area to make up for a lack of ability in another.
2. Projection – The process of attributing one's own intolerable emotional feelings to another; perceiving and calling attention to

undesirable traits in others to avoid dealing with the same deficiencies in one's self.

3. Rationalization – A conscious attempt to explain away or justify something unacceptable by giving seemingly good reasons.

4. Regression – The process of returning to a less symbolic fashion or to an earlier level of achievement as a child.

5. Repression – The ability to forget anything that is distasteful or intolerable and to ignore the memory of painful experiences.

6. Suppression – When you push away thoughts or feelings that are undesirable or make you uncomfortable, you are suppressing them.

7. Restitution – To avoid accepting wrong-doing, one may attempt to make up for hurtful actions by being nice, buying gifts, or doing special things with the person who has been wronged.

8. Denial – A tool used to avoid feeling pain by believing nothing has happened or refusing to accept responsibility for one's actions is a form of denial.

9. Negativism – Ignoring the existence of a problem by resorting to such reactions as stubbornness and rebellion against authority is a form of negative behavior. It serves as a protection against feelings of cowardice and inadequacy. In many instances, the negative individual refuses to do anything about the problem.

10. Perfectionism – Attempting to escape blame or criticism by performing perfectly is an impossible endeavor, yet these people may feel justified in pointing out the imperfections of others as a way to divert attention from their own inadequacies.

If you feel wounded and use any of the above devices, you may want to reflect on Revelations, chapters two and three. To move into healing through God's ways, you need to confront your past and identify and understand the conflict. "He that hath an ear, let him hear what the Spirit saith unto the churches; To him that overcometh will I give to eat of the tree of life, which is in the midst of the paradise of God" (Revelation 2:7).

Many people attempt to use religion as a crutch in order to avoid feelings of fear, uncertainty, and anger. There is a difference between having a real relationship with God and using religion as a quick fix. Make sure you examine your heart and your relationship with Jesus. It's vital to be completely honest with yourself regarding these matters.

A TIME TO REFLECT:

1. In what ways do you need to prepare
    yourself to accept the challenge to think like
    God?

    _____

    _____

    _____

2. What coping mechanisms do you rely on to
    deal with stress or conflict?

    _____

    _____

    _____

    _____

3. What are some God-like, healthier ways to
    handle your stressors?

    _____

    _____

    _____

    _____

4. What creative things can you do to minimize your daily stress?

_____

_____

_____

_____

5. What dreams do you believe God has placed in your heart? (Remember, no dream is too big or too small for God.)

_____

_____

_____

_____

REPEAT THE RESOLUTION:

I resolve to change and live in the Law of Original Intent and Dream the Dreams of God. I resolve to work on restoring my mind, my spiritual sensitivity, and the original me. I resolve to identity my blind spots and the enemy inside me.

CHAPTER 5

CHALLENGED TO BE RISEN BY DECISION: ADVERSITY IS THE FATHER OF MENTAL TOUGHNESS

This process of change, transformation, and maturation requires a decision that even when life knocks you down and you fall, you will get up and win. Adversity happens to everyone, and it happens all the time. You cannot expect life to be perfect, and if you understand this, then you'll be able to avoid the impulse to quit. Even if you are strong enough to persist through the obstacle course of life, sometimes, you will encounter an adverse event that will completely knock you on your back.

Dad loved boxing, and our family attended live boxing matches featuring one of the sport's greatest champions, Cassius Clay (Mohammed Ali). We loved to observe champions and identify their strategies over their opponents. Daddy taught us how to box and gave us strategies to toughen us up as young children. We used punching bags and boxing gloves to learn how to fight. When challenged, we knew how to win. We learned the art of fighting, but not the science of critical thinking. During our education, we learned the three R's: reading, writing, arithmetic, but not the art of managing our emotions.

It is one thing to know how to fight using your body, but it's another thing to fight using your spirit. Daddy was always by my side when he taught me about boxing. Likewise, God is always by your side when you come across spiritual warfare. You may not be able to see Him, but if you concentrate, He will make His presence known to you as you stand in your spiritual armor.

SELF-SABOTAGE IS FIGHTING A SPIRITUAL BATTLE IN THE NATURAL

One of the major tools Satan uses is self-sabotage. He weakens your resolve by planting lies in your head. If you hear that you are a failure or no good enough times, soon, you will believe it.

Defensive mechanisms may cause children to be shamed because they labor under unrealistic expectations and feel they never live up to those expectations. Defense mechanisms deny problems, hide the pain, and maintain illusions that become delusions and conclusions.

Many people spend most of their energy trying to maintain a certain image rather than figuring out how to solve problems. Often, children learn to be ashamed of their emotions and feelings. They even may deny that they feel emotions. When they stuff their feelings deep inside on a regular basis, they are buried alive, never able to go anywhere but implode and explode at the most inappropriate times. A child is devalued when the family considers emotions worthless.

Children now take on what should be their parents' responsibilities by facing challenges alone in order to hide while maintaining a certain image.

When relationships become distant and disconnected, you may learn how to go through the motions of intimacy. When your mind, body, soul, and spirit work at against one another, it's easy to overreact, to give in to negative thoughts, and live in anger, therefore creating an unhealthy balance.

Your mind seeks to explain, create, and control. Your body craves to experience, accomplish, and grow. Your heart yearns to attach, give, and feel, which can result in anxiety.

Cain and Abel modeled sibling rivalry based on parental preferences. Ninety-six percent of families are, to some degree, emotionally impaired by the unhealthy rules passed on from one generation to another. Our society is sick because our families are sick, and our families are sick because we are living by inherited rules that God never wrote.

ATTACHMENT STYLES DESCRIBE
RELATIONSHIP DYNAMICS

Unarguably, the healthiest of these attachment style personalities is the secure-attachment style. These people feel comfortable in their skins. This allows them to venture out into the world by themselves. They don't feel the need to cling to others, and they allow the people in their lives to be independent. When people around them feel stressed, secure-attachment personalities are able to offer comfort.

The avoidant-attachment style avoids intimacy and dampens emotions in personal relationships. Closeness brings fear of rejection, so the person remains on the periphery of intimacy and attaches to things and success. This defense ultimately destroys the true bond of love that can exist between two people.

The ambivalent-attachment style personality does the opposite. These people seek intimacy but grab for it too tightly. They may exchange "addictive attachments" over genuine involvement, love, and concern. They may deeply believe that if they can hold on tightly enough, they can avoid separations and, ultimately, even death. Unfortunately, this defense can lead to feelings of alienation and loneliness.

The disorganized-attachment style may use the avoidant or ambivalent response or even a mixture of both. These people also tend to go numb, feeling as if the world around them is not real. Often, their children are terrified of their parents, but have a longing and yearning to be nurtured by them.

An anxious-attachment style personality compels a person to be near loved ones all the time. When separated, they tend to feel anxious and out of control. In order to achieve this, they may isolate the person they feel attached to or they may select someone whom others have a hard time making a connection with.

There is a thief in the house, but if you catch him, he has to repay you sevenfold. Why don't you resolve to recover your identity, purpose, life, and attitude?

For at least ten years, God echoed the word *resolve* in my spirit. I meditated on it, and God said, "You must come to a definite or earnest decision in the very essence and core of your being. Who will you serve: God or materialistic things?"

The process begins the moment you start to choose or think about winning. The process of learning, however, is always the same, no matter what the subject. First, you make mistakes and experience some failures until your subconscious mind learns by trial and error and practice, practice, practice. Every time you are willing to try again, it becomes easier until eventually you realize you have developed a new skillset.

Dr. Joyce Baldwin is a profound educator who serves my community as a principal. She and her husband, Elder Charles Baldwin, raised and developed two children who are also great leaders.

She taught spiritual skillsets to expose the enemy and spiritual strategies to overcome. I attended one of her seminars, *Arise,* during a women's retreat. She provided the practical application and reinforced the importance of decision-making in order to accomplish change. First, I needed to identify my ambivalent attachment relationships. These are relationships where I found myself becoming reluctant to develop close connections with others. I'd often worry that people may not love me, and when a relationship ended, I became upset, almost inconsolable. I decided I didn't want to live that way anymore, so I used the principles she taught to develop secure attachment relationships. I learned how to let others into my inner circle. I realized that I needed to be able to depend on and trust others. I wanted to interact with people and feel secure in knowing who I am. The first step is realizing that Satan doesn't want you to know who you are. He wants you to be blinded to who you are and to the work you are capable of accomplishing.

There are different ways an enemy can steal your identity. Of course, you've heard about identify theft and criminals who want to get your vital statistics in order to live the high life. Satan operates in a similar fashion. Sometimes, he may whisper malicious lies in your ear that make you wish you could be like someone else. However, God formed you before the foundation of the world, and if you yearn to be someone other than the person whom He created you to be, you are trying to take away God's glory.

Satan wants to steal your identity because he realizes your benefit to the Kingdom of God. Therefore, he tries to confuse you. He has many different strategies to take you down.

a. Power Punches – Punches that knock somebody out. It's a straight right, a forceful blow that results from major disappointments from mistakes you have made or life-altering circumstances such as the death of a loved one. If you don't feel accepted or worthy, that punch can knock you off your feet and take you out of the match, confusing you as to whom you really are.

b. Hook – The left hook comes from the inside, when you're right next to your nemesis. It's likened to the damage done by someone who you thought was a friend. It's hard for someone who is not close to hurt you, but children, good friends, family members, or someone you thought was a loyal employee could betray you.

c. Upper Cut – The goal is to pound the middle of the chest. These blows often result in a broken heart, leaving you feeling crippled and alone.

d. Jab – The enemy's busiest and most effective weapon is the jab. He uses short hits and punches. It won't be a knock out, but right before a major thing happens, jabs are being thrown at you. Soon, your defenses become battered down. The devil's desire is to make you give up the fight and stop believing in yourself; it causes considerable damage. The jabs are lies from the deceiver because he doesn't want you to believe you are made in the wonderful and beautiful image of God.

These hits can cause you to lose faith in your abilities and your value. Instead of discerning positive qualities, you may begin to label negative traits. The danger of labeling, and often every negative trait, is that the positive quality is misused.

For example, the words conceited, talkative, overbearing, or arrogant are negative labels, but in reality, these can actually be traits of a confident person.

It is important not to believe the toxic statements. People say poisonous statements and can make you second-guess yourself. It takes hundreds, if not thousands, of positive statements to cancel out one negative statement. Self-criticism can be extremely brutal and irrational, and little things do become big things as you scream at yourself.

Examine your critical thoughts and the reasoning behind them, especially if they cause you to beat yourself up; the little foxes are chipping away at you.

If you have thought about who you are and what your purpose in life is, I urge you to study Ephesians 6. You are a Christian soldier – engaged in warfare, not in a natural fight but a spiritual onslaught from the devil. You put on the armor of God so that you may be able to stand against the wiles of the devil.

Rise to the challenge; establish a training regimen. Repetition is to rehearse and repeat scriptures and affirmation statements. Here are a few to get you started:

"I can do all things through Christ which strengtheneth me." Philippians 4:13

"No weapon that is formed against thee shall prosper; and every tongue that shall rise against thee in judgment thou shalt condemn. This is the heritage of the servants of the Lord, and their righteousness is of me, saith the Lord." Isaiah 54:17

"And we know that all things work together for good to them that love God, to them who are the called according to his purpose." Romans 8:28

Stretching--Look at the great masterpiece that God made; you are a stunning delight. You have to stretch out on God, believing who He is, and believe God can handle any problem.

Dream big and in color; what do you want to be when you grow up? You can't use the excuse, "I'm too old or too young to dream." Nutrition is essential to healthy lifestyles. Eat right and stay strong; you need food for strength.

Shadow box – When boxers shadow box, they pretend they are fighting someone else. They get disappointed and believe that they will not get to box other opponents. This time, it's going to happen again. You are boxing against yourself. If you're doing your best at any given moment in time, that is all anyone can ask of you. You're likely your own worst critic. Remember your best changes from day to day. Don't live in the past, comparing your present self to a shadow of who you once were. Today, do your best.

Sparring practice – You must partner with the positive people who will celebrate you now, even though the numbers may be small.

Everyone can't be in the front row. Be careful and pick your associates wisely. The people around you are one of the greatest dangers to knowing who you are. When sparring, find people who celebrate you.

Often, you'll discover that your personality will mimic those around you. You can't have haters in your front row; every time you excel, haters will try to knock you down. You don't need sarcastic people criticizing your achievements and making you question your value. It is vital to make sure you don't have enemies calling you names.

Work on building up your positive attributes. In today's world, people tend to focus on the negative aspects of life. Don't let people get you tied up on your weaknesses. Ministry is every Christian's assignment from God, but your gift is something that is unique to you. There is no greater purpose than what God has intended for your life.

Allow every cell in your body to participate in worship. When you worship, you become closer to Jesus. When the enemy comes, you must be able to recognize him because it's easier to confront him when you know who he is.

Elevation - The higher you rise, the farther you get from the bottom where the foxes come in and attempt to destroy you. The devil's former tools will no longer be adequate. Do not give the anticipated reaction to the devil because he will know the toxic things to fight. When you are risen by decision, you become more than a conqueror. You have won before you began because you have God on your side. The boxer in the corner is beaten down, and his trainer provides water and tells him to get up. If you want to win, you must get up.

God will help you and hide you in a safe place. During my boxing match with the devil, hits came from the left and right, but Jesus gave me the ability to punch him right back. Because Jesus was by my side, I won that boxing match against my enemy.

Psalm 57 states the enemy is going to fight us, but we're under the shadow of God's wings, and He makes refuge for us as the Kingdom of God awaits us.

There is a huge difference in who you are and what you do. Because of the challenge, it's difficult for some to see their greatness. God has a purpose for your life and will not allow anyone to change the true essence of who you are. Never allow the enemy to convince you that you're anything less than who you are.

If you apply the following acronyms to your daily life, you'll be able to rise up and meet Jesus.

RISEN BY DECISION

R - REDUCE

Reduce stress by learning new life skills.

Reduce substance use to cope with pain.

Reduce toxic relationships.

I – INCREASE

Increase your self- awareness and learn how to affect and interact with people.

Increase your awareness of feelings.

Increase your understanding of yourself and why you do what you do.

Increase assertiveness, which can draw the right people closer to you.

Increase the healthy influences in your life.

Increase time alone with God in Bible study and prayer.

S –SUBSTITUTE

Substitute positive emotions for negative ones.

Substitute willingness to risk for fear and procrastination.

Substitute humility for arrogance.

Substitute acceptance for anger.

Substitute peace for anxiety.

Substitute surrender for control.

E – ELIMINATE

Eliminate addictive behavior.

Eliminate a critical and judgmental spirit.

Eliminate a certain repetitive cycle of sin in your life.

Eliminate non-forgiveness.

Eliminate resentment.

Adversity often causes you to start doubting yourself, yet you must choose to combat that doubt by maintaining focus on your purpose. When doubt sets in, panic starts to set in; however, that's when you need to revisit your core beliefs. Allow the spirit within to guide you and reroute you onto the right path, the right strategies, and the right decisions. When you trust God to fight your battles, He will give you the strategies you need to participate in His plan.

You must have faith and unwavering resolve in God. You are learning to handle yourself with integrity in tough times because your value is not seen when everything is going well. Instead, it is displayed during adversities by your ability to get up and keep moving in peace, joy, and righteousness.

How do you overcome illness, tragedy, and loss of others? These parts of life are the toughest. Make decisions to move on by changing your attitude from pointless negativity and learn to appreciate the good. Refocus on what you have today, rather than what you lost yesterday. There is a continual reframing, refocusing, restoring and renewing process. This is part of life's mystery. Acceptance is the key to returning to your life while making adjustments to proceed forward without the person, place, or thing that bogged you down originally.

God is my gracious Father. When Daddy took a turn for the worse, I clearly heard God speak to me at 10:00 a.m. "Call home and check on your dad."

I thought, *I just called a little while ago and he didn't feel like talking then. There's no point in trying to call him again now. I'll just end up getting my feelings hurt again and I can't handle any more rejection today. He's going to say, "Cheryl, get a life and quit calling me so much." I'll call him tomorrow.* My disobedience taught me a valuable lesson.

I left to run some errands, and when I returned home, my stomach plummeted when I heard the message my brother, Butch, left me. "Cheryl, we had to take Dad back to the hospital, and he has pneumonia."

God gently and lovingly spoke, "I'm going to take your Dad, and I want you to accept it." God prepared me for His will and left me to decide if I would trust Him with all my heart to carry me through my grief.

I am grateful that my father reflected the life he shared with us, even up to his death. He said, "I've lived my life; I made the choice to smoke cigarettes since I was nine years old, and I'm not afraid to die. I choose to go with whatever they found in my body. I'm proud of you guys, and your mother is a great woman."

I was blessed to watch with my mother and the beauty of my Dad's last choice in the adversities in his life. He closed his eyes at bedtime, turned his head, and died. He fought multiple illnesses for sixteen years. He fought a great fight. By sharing stories from his deplorable childhood, he taught me that I must be mentally tough. Dad never lied. He taught me that life is tough, and I strive to honor his memory, legacy, and example.

My father's last wish for his five children was for us to take good care of Mama and love and support each other. We are a work in progress. We are still learning to make the adjustments for one another's temperament and personality.

The founder of L.I.F.E. said, "You can never say that you didn't get anything out of L.I.F.E. When you can share with others that you have a healthy marriage, you are able to pay your debts, you are acquiring skillsets to heal relationships, or you have a support team of smiley, happy, shiny people, you did benefit; even if you're not rich, you are wealthy." Winners never quit. Quitters never win. I am living an abundant life.

A TIME TO REFLECT:

1. What image do you try to maintain and why?

   _____

   _____

   _____

   _____

   _____

2. What type of attachment styles do you use in most of your relationships and why?
   (Secure, Avoidance, Ambivalence, Disorganized, Anxious)

   _____

   _____

   _____

   _____

   _____

3. What defense mechanisms do you rely on regularly?

   _____

   _____

_____

_____

_____

_____

4. What can you do to replace unhealthy
   mechanisms with healthy ones?

_____

_____

_____

_____

5. In what ways has Satan tried to attack you
   recently?

_____

_____

_____

_____

6. What lies does Satan whisper in your ears?

_____

_____

_____

_____

_____

_____

_____

7. What truths can you use to replace the lies?

_____

_____

_____

_____

_____

_____

_____

8. Describe a time when you disobeyed God, and what have you learned from that experience?

_____

_____

_____

_____

_____

REPEAT THE RESOLUTION:

I resolve to rise above adversities by making Godly decisions. I resolve to develop my spiritual and social-psychological muscles.

CHAPTER 6

CHALLENGED TO BELIEVE THIS IS A BLESSING: I'M TOO BLESSED TO BE STRESSED

Your greatest strength can also be your greatest weakness. Job was tested because of his faith in God, not because of his lack of faith. His faith caused God to present him to Satan to challenge his position and posture in God. Job was an upright, mature, and righteous man and a credit to his community. He was a wealthy man and loved his family. Life can't get any better than that.

Adversities in life are blessings. The quality of joy is determined by the quality of sorrow. Never make life-changing decisions during times of sickness, fatigue, anger, loneliness, or hunger.

Decisions determine your destiny. When you make decisions with partial information, you can make bad choices and experience painful, unexpected consequences. You need the sight of

God, insight, and foresight to perceive direction and information in order to walk in the light.

It was difficult for me to comprehend the process of critical thinking during Bible study because I experienced bouts of chemical imbalances and fluctuating blood sugar. Challenged to focus on studying and reading the Bible, my strongest Christian disciplines were prayer and fasting. I was able to take any negativity and cast it to God. I love to worship God for hours. It is wonderful to be lost in His presence.

God is not trying to destroy you. St. John 1:11 states, "Whatever God begins in pain always ends with power." God never breaks you without making you, and God never makes you without breaking you. Do you really believe this in your heart? Your answer often may depend upon which resource you use: God's Words, Satan's lies, or your own distorted perception and irrational thoughts. At best, communication is challenging when you don't understand the truth. Because of my chemical imbalance, it was difficult to focus, and my comprehension of the truth was weak without consistent Bible study.

Apostle Paul learned to view pain, suffering, and brokenness through God's perspective. God gave Paul spiritual insight that far surpassed anything he had known. God allowed Paul to be buffeted by a thorn in his side and severe trials in order to humble him and remove the potential for pride.

In 2 Corinthians 12:7, Paul talks about his thorn. "And lest I should be exalted above measure through the abundance of the revelations, there was given to me a thorn in the flesh, the messenger of Satan to buffet me, lest I should be exalted above measure." Observe Paul through his time of weakness. He learned a new and unexpected principle. *Weakness is strength.* Frailty in a certain area should never bring embarrassment. Whatever brings you to your knees in weakness carries the greatest potential for your personal success and victory.

When you accept your weakness and the fact that you cannot handle life on your own, God goes to work. He sends encouragement and a sense of creativity, helping you to try new avenues that lead to hope and fresh beginnings. You are struck with a defining thought: *I need God.*

In Hebrews 10:35-36, it states, "We cannot cast away our confidence in God which has a great reward. For we have need of endurance, so that after we have done the will of God, we may receive the promise." Look to God, the author and finisher of your faith, so you can be His witness to encourage and observe others, not to throw away their confidence because of their circumstances.

Secondly, you need to affirm your commitment to Him that you will remain focused.

Most people, including Christians, refuse to be broken. You can never be used by God at your finest if you refuse the most crucial process in your journey to your destiny. St. John 12:24 states, "Except a corn of wheat falls into the ground and dies, it abides alone: but if it dies, it brings forth much fruit." Jesus fell into the ground and died as a seed, and when resurrected, He was The Bread of Life. He carried His cross so that you would learn to carry the crosses you must bear in life.

Pain is an equal opportunity employer; it does not discriminate by race, social status, religion, or denomination. Christians know that Christ learned obedience by the things He suffered. Pain is inevitable, but misery is optional. Perception is stronger than the truth unless you renew your mind daily.

The purpose of any pain is to identify it as an indicator or a warning that imminent disease, mental affliction, or spiritual apathy is near. Pain paves the way to face hidden agendas and heal the inner person, preventing stress-related illnesses, sudden deaths, and disconnection from spiritual connectors.

During the preparation for Luther's and my Sweetest Day weekend, I heard God speak, "Cancel your plans for today and spend some quality time with me."

I thought He was preparing me to minister in Toronto, Canada and giving me His mind for their women's retreat.

After several hours in God's presence, I noticed pain, redness, and swelling in my right calf. I went to the local emergency department, and the doctor discovered a blood clot. The doctors immediately transported me by ambulance and admitted me at a bigger hospital for five days.

After my discharge, I became a couch potato for two months in order to prevent the blood clot from travelling through my veins into my brain or lungs, which had the potential to be fatal. Shut in from attending church, councils, conventions, and some leadership conferences was seemingly the end of the ministry; I was devastated. I asked God, "What did I do to displease you, Lord?"

He answered, "Just as Job was buffeted by Satan without a cause, I asked Satan, 'Have you considered my servant, Cheryl?' "

I imagined the angels encouraging me as if they were celebrating my victory. I wasn't challenged because I did something wrong--quite the contrary; I had made an earnest and sincere decision to change and walk by faith and not by sight. My faith was on trial.

God used the pain as a warning, and it was a miracle that I could hear His voice. If I had disobeyed God and gone shopping, I would have shopped until I dropped, literally. I praise God for His grace and love because He is the potter and I am the clay. He is sovereign, and His Way is the right way.

Yes, you may feel dizzy as you spin on His wheel, day after day. Just when you process through, ready to receive the finishing touches, there is another lump. BAM! BAM! SLAM! SLAM! You are slapped on the table and broken again.

You may find yourself asking, "How many times do I need to be broken?"

My answer to you is quite simple: "Until you become smart enough to recognize that you are not God and He purchased you with His love. God corrects, challenges, and changes into better beings those whom He loves."

In retrospect, I appreciate every broken piece in my life. Thirty-eight years, ago, I asked, "Why me?" The cry and plight of a victim is always self-focused. When I made right decisions, as a victor, I perceived my challenges as blessings.

Thirty-three years earlier, Dr. Deloisteen Brown admitted me to St. Joseph Hospital in Ann Arbor, Michigan during the Thanksgiving holiday season in 1980. I was diagnosed with severe malnutrition, chronic clinical depression, and anxiety neurosis. I was told I'd be like a baby for five years and would have to learn how to walk, talk, eat, and think again.

After ten days, the social worker confronted me with two choices upon discharge: Shawnie and I could move to a battered women's shelter or become intensely involved in vocational rehabilitation services with the support of the community and my church, Messiah's Temple, in Ypsilanti, Michigan. The decision was unanimous;

the church members said, "Send her home with us, and we will take good care of her." My family travelled to Ypsilanti frequently to support us.

The networking within the community was the love that I was looking for because I was ushered right into the face of God. My friend, Jewell, wheeled me out of the hospital and transported me into my cousin's car; friends carried me into the house. Unable to walk, talk, think, eat, cook, or function, my eleven-year-old daughter, Shawnie, would help me down the stairs and sit me on the red velvet couch. When I needed to go up or down the steps, I would crawl up and scoot down. I won a scholarship from the Counseling Center, Natural Growth, to attend monthly retreats for holistic healing in the quiet, remote woods in Dexter, Michigan. The beauty of quiet yields great rewards of rest and renews confidence. I was taught natural detoxification, healthy lifestyle changes in eating and food choices, and exercise.

I learned alternative approaches to manage my chronic clinical pain, exercise my psychological muscles, and reduce the use of some medications. Pain causes a cycle of physical changes. When my pain flared, I experienced reduced flexibility, inactivity, loss of strength, and deconditioning. Pain also caused a cycle of emotional stressors of depression, isolation, anxiety and anger. The pain cycle for psychosocial stressors diminished the quality of my life. I couldn't work; I experienced reduced support, conflict, and economic stress. I learned a new method of walking to strengthen the weakness in the body. My steps are different now, but life hurts.

There I met college professors, doctors, lawyers, wives, and devastated divorcées. I was shocked. I had thought pain and devastation only happened to Blacks, yet here I was one of three Blacks, amongst Michigan's elite, attending monthly retreats for two years. Even though I'd received a Bachelor's Degree in Sociology and a Master's Degree in Guidance and Counseling, the most significant achievement was my salvation and the Biblical principles I learned at church. I was a

Christian, learning valuable life skills for emotional healing.

I asked, "Why me?" I learned my question should have been, "Why not me?" Bad things happen to everyone. Being a Christian didn't exempt me from pain, but the bumpy road was easier to travel with Jesus by my side. My life-script began to unfold one night. The leaders asked us to perform in an impromptu talent show in ten minutes. Thoughts battered my mind as my body trembled in rebellion. *Oh my God, what do I do? I can't sing, dance or tell jokes. Please, God, help me.*

In response to my prayer, God's reply thundered in my ears. "Tell them about Me, how I am your shepherd, and how you learned your greatest lessons in the valley." My God had never left me nor forsaken me. That sermon became the first of many where I would have the blessing of ministering to hurting souls for a period covering over thirty years.

I had never imagined that God's call into the ministry would be a tedious journey for me. I needed to learn how to become an efficient leader, but first I needed to understand what made me a good follower. The following is my translation of the beloved and well-known psalm. The parts in italics come from the New King James Version to Psalm 23.

PSALM 23

The Lord is my Shepherd = Relationship

I shall not want = Supply

He makes me to lie down in green pastures = Rest

He leads me beside the still waters = Refreshment.

He restores my soul = Healing.

He leads me in the paths of righteousness = Guidance.

For His name's sake = Purpose.

Yea, though I walk through the valley of the shadow of death = Trials

I will fear no evil = Protection.

For Thou art with me = Faithfulness.

Thy rod and Thy staff they comfort me = Discipline.

Thou prepare a table before me in the presence of mine enemies = Hope.

Thou anoints my head with oil = Consecration.

My cup runs over = Abundance.

Surely goodness and mercy shall follow me all the days of my life = Blessings.

*And I will dwell in the house of the Lor*d = Security.

Forever = Eternity.

What is most valuable? It is not what you have in your life, but *whom* you have in your life.

"Do not ask the Lord to guide your footsteps if you are not willing to move your feet" (Author Unknown).

Difficulties of life are not the plans of a hard-hearted God, but rather products of life that God intends to use to make you strong. Brokenness is not evidence of God's absence, as many so often perceive, but of God's presence. Feelings of brokenness do not come from God; however, The

Good Shepherd uses these tribulations to strengthen His beloved sheep. Brokenness is a solemn time when God explains the contradictions you see every day. It is at this time that you must be still and know God; otherwise, you may miss the critical peace and timing of God's restorative work in you. God, in His redemptive role, delivered you from the judgment of sin. However, the memory and removal of the sin, as well as the immoral patterns of life, are the obstacles that hinder the Spirit's work. It is your responsibility, through the guidance from God and participation with God, to embrace pain.

He shows you the truth about yourself and gives you the grace to come before Him and heal. You can't heal what you don't feel. You can rebuild, however, through the process of brokenness because you cannot ignore your hunger for love and wholeness. He wants you to find the pain; face the pain; and fix the pain.

God breaks the defense mechanisms in your soul that you have created in order to protect yourself from pain. Then God delivers you from unhealed hurts, irrational thinking, hardened perceptions, and debilitating behaviors. You need to learn how to redefine the truth of the words you've believed by removing the labels that have paralyzed you for years, and by identifying the original lies that you have believed about yourself and others.

I learned a great deal when I read Dr. Brenda Wade's book, *What Mama Couldn't Tell Us about Love: Healing the Emotional Legacy of Racism by Celebrating Our Light.* Many people don't fully understand the power certain lies or misconceptions can have on a person. Often, people see a strong woman as someone who doesn't need any help from others. However, Ms. Wade believes a strong female focuses on her emotions and makes her needs known in order to fulfill them. Be careful not to follow the slave mentality of your forbearers. Many women would subconsciously avoid seeking out the source of their pain. They may have had a certain way of thinking that affected relationships with others. A manifestation of anger can be depression.

Many Black women don't vocalize their depression with the words, "I feel sad." Instead, it has become a stereotype of the Black women instead to say, "I'm mad." Because of their history, African-Americans had to stifle their emotions; modern females may have been encoded to do the same. If you come across an angry Black woman, stop and take a moment to decipher if she is actually angry or perhaps masking her depression through inappropriate words and actions. Many are upset because their family and friends may define asking for help as a sign of weakness. It became a way of life in order for the Black women to survive. Many tell themselves, "Carry on no matter what. Stop looking like a crazy person; instead, focus on maintaining a prestigious or wealthy lifestyle."

After experiencing a nervous breakdown over thirty years ago, I began breaking the cycle of an intergenerational trauma, which caused me to become aware of the barrier to generational blessings. The women in my family are strong-willed with unassuming masks. Our gene pool deposited over-sensitive, fragile, and obsessive traits. We were expert caregivers who specialized in being strong (and sometimes wrong), determined, and bossy.

Something happens when women assume caregiving roles too soon in life. When the root of giving and caring is driven by deep pain and loss, whatever drives them controls them. The root of the defense of stubbornness is a belief that they are right and know what's best as they protect others. Their core values really express the neediness and cries for help from controlling spirits. Warfare within negates the ability to access God quickly, but perceives the love of a man is more important because girls are raised to become wives and mothers.

When the women's biological time clocks fiercely rear their ugly heads, some females may make desperate attempts to control their own destiny. Some may withdraw and become prey to a controlling person to make their decisions so they feel protected, only to discover their neediness. Looking for love in the wrong places allows Satan and his dressed-up lies to lower them into the Kingdom of Man and demonic realms.

They are fighting, carrying their stubbornness and ambivalent attachment into spiritual warfare with natural, carnal weapons. They allow the enemy access to their minds, and he wears them down and reduces them to lower standards of life, existing and struggling from day to day.

The unconditional love of God using family and friends allowed me to begin to heal from "a shadow." Silence is golden in God. Psalm 46:10 states, "Be still and know that I am God..." In other words, quit holding on to everything that keeps you from hearing God's direction and assurance. This solitude, silence, and stillness revealed insight and answers. I remember asking, "Why am I broke and on welfare with a master's degree? Why do I have chronic physical ailments? Why do I feel so drained, tired and exhausted most of the time?"

My body began to talk back to me, and as I listened, I began to defy the cultural traditions that resisted receiving help and getting my needs met. I began to take advantage of the times I live in, which provide mental-health services to help me heal. I redefined the word "strength" to mean "I really do have feelings; I have needs and am going to allow God to lead me to the people, agencies, institutions, facilities, and churches to meet them."

I began a disciplined exercise program and changed my diet to fruits and vegetables for a season. The body is the temple of the soul. I actually felt the toxins and poison in my body leave my brain. You have to love and honor the temple first because if the basic needs of food and shelter are unmet, it becomes difficult to hear spiritual truths.

During this season of self-discovery, others chastised me because the church was the sole resource for families to resolve their conflicts. Women came up to me and said, "We don't share family secrets. What goes on in the house stays in the house." The truth is that the more secrets I revealed, the more sicknesses God healed.

Seeking to attack the original lies was difficult, until God commanded, "Cheryl, you must stop living a lie." I finally discerned what He was saying and began to discover the hidden lies in my original core that were piled on top of the truth. These lies hid in my subconscious and unconscious mind. Without the conscious, subconscious, and unconscious mind being in alignment, it is difficult to live life in the present. You will become chained to the past or feel anxious about your future.

One lie was replaced with the truth of God's Word, and then the immediate obedience to act and apply the revealed truth began to release me into His presence. When your eyes are finally opened to the consequences, even though you may blame others for your misery and pain, the truth is what heals you and helps you to live a spirit-led life rather than just spirit-filled lives. You can pray the following prayer each day to help you stay focused:

Lord, open my eyes that I might see you and know your will.

The thief really blinded me. He embezzled property that was entrusted to my care. Every time you fail to watch and pray, Satan opens the door to sin, and he obtains unlawful entry into your mind. This thief then alters or distorts God's word and perception.

Now, any problem can lead you to discover who you are, who God is, who your true friends are, and who your enemies are as you continue the journey to resolution. The process that challenges most Christians is the denial of the broken, distorted image of self. My first book, *Broken to Be Made Whole,* was written by the breath of God to identify the undeveloped areas of your mind and renew them daily. The Word of God and attending church regularly has healed many Christians. Depending on the degree of family dysfunction, others may require divine intervention, deliverance, miracles, or exorcism.

The late Norman L. Wagner, who was my pastor for years, believed that the Bible and the act of laying on hands would deliver Christians from Satan. There are some, however, who must stay in God's Word, stay at the altar in prayer, have a strong mentor, take their medicine, and seek a spirit-filled counselor. I am grateful that I heard my pastor utter those words of release for some who must participate with God in tailor-made healing, in spite of the doubts of others who are blessed to live solely by Biblical principles. This breaking and making process connects you to your sin, stubbornness, or insensitivity to God. It reveals an area of unreleased control that seeks control as a Sovereign God. When you have the spirit of infirmity that exists for years, it is the indicator that this is a generational curse; however, once Jesus delivers you, you are blessed.

Remember, the answers to your questions often depend upon which resource you use, God's Truths, Satan's lies, or your own distorted perceptions and irrational thought patterns. Your challenge will become a blessing when you believe God and know His truths.

A TIME TO REFLECT:

1. What are your greatest strengths and greatest
   weaknesses?

   _____

   _____

   _____

   _____

   _____

2. What are three life-defining decisions you
   have made in the past and how have they
   defined who you are today?

   _____

   _____

   _____

   _____

   _____

3. In what ways, if any, would you change
   those past decisions and why?

   _____

   _____

   _____

_____

_____

4. When have you been tempted to disobey
    God, and what was the outcome?

    _____

    _____

    _____

    _____

    _____

5. When have you been a victim, and what
    could you have done to become a victor?

    _____

    _____

    _____

    _____

    _____

    _____

7. What does the word strength mean to you?

    _____

    _____

    _____

    _____

REPEAT THE RESOLUTION:

I resolve to perceive challenges as blessings. I'm too blessed to be stressed. I accept the challenge to make the right decisions.

CHAPTER 7

CHALLENGED TO CHOOSE:
THERE ARE TWO OF YOU

Choose this day whom you will serve, God or greed. Choose life or death. The Bible is full of ultimatums where you must choose. Do you accept the challenge to choose life?

Either you can own your choices in life or others will make choices for you. Even though some experiences aren't good, they do work together for your good if you choose to seek God. The consequences will be evident in your personality, attitude, and posture in life. When you resist, God knows how to wait until you choose to become like Him.

You may encounter major attacks when you resolve in your heart to change. However, these attacks are used by God to build inner strength, fortitude, character, and a strong resolve.

Elder Craig Gilchrist, a preacher in His own right, taught me the five major attacks.

1. The Call

We lack the ability to comprehend God's voice when he calls us. "Follow me and I will make you fishers of men."

2. Identity

We lost our minds and identities during the fall in the Garden of Eden and haven't chosen to feel upstanding and worthy to be blessed because we don't know who we are.

3. Character

We sometimes lack the ability to be consistent in who we really are, and because of our inconsistencies it's difficult to maintain and sustain our spiritual maturity.

4. Resources

We struggle with energy and the inner resources, resolve and abilities to bring forth our destiny.

5. God

We have power and authority over Satan's limited authority as the prince of power over the air waves and darkness. Yet, we become victims under his only power, deception, as he uses the art of manipulation and intimidation.

My consequences for resisting resulted in the past repeating over and over. I felt as if I was going in circles, bending over, and sweeping more fragments with the broom, and then I kept shoveling those fragments into the dustpan. While throwing these broken pieces into the garbage, I thought, *I'm getting too old to keep struggling because I am resisting change.*

In this day and time, the Apostolic anointing is needed to change the atmosphere for God in the earth. Apostolic anointing is not a denomination but a calling to minister to others; it requires transition, transformation, and change. Change is inevitable, and it is the stable constant in life.

God is so patient, kind, gracious, generous, loving, faithful, merciful, wonderful, patient, longsuffering, and wise. He waits for you to make the choice to change, then He makes the necessary changes. He is not trying to change who He created you to be. He's been waiting for you to discover and know who you are; know Him who created you; know your friends who supported you; and know the enemy who distorted you.

My son-in-law, Elder David Thompson, Chief Probation Officer for the Municipal Court in Youngstown, Ohio, preached a profound message. "Change can be the most difficult challenge you may ever encounter in your life. Most people never change because they don't have what it takes to meet the challenge and sustain the process. To change a lifestyle or a habit is not an event, but a process filled with many seeming failures as well as successes.

Change is recovery from a certain debilitating lifestyle pattern. Everyone has his or her own particular configurations based upon genetic makeup and environment. Recovery involves taking back the original control which was lost in the debilitating lifestyle that was adopted to protect oneself from perceived, real, or imagined hurt that has now outdated itself in one's life.

Most people are willing to accept their present reality and even the insanity of their reality rather than accepting the opportunity to modify themselves and reach out and grab the promises of their possibilities."

David wanted to change, and he tried, but it didn't work. In the Urban Dictionary, insanity is defined as doing the same things repeatedly and expecting different results. If you want to change your life, yet you repeat the same habits and keep company with the same people, you will become frustrated, unfulfilled, and disillusioned when your dreams do not become a reality and your promises do not manifest.

If you are living a life of problem after problem, you'll feel defeated quite quickly. You may have uttered the phrase, "Life isn't fair." Actually, that statement is true; however, there is nothing you can do about it. Truthfully, you should be quite grateful that life isn't fair because Jesus died for you to live in Heaven with Him forever. If life were truly just, you would be destined to an eternity in Hell. *Thank you, Jesus, for loving us enough to spare us.* There are many injustices in the world over which you have no control; however, you do have the ability to change some aspects of your life. If you do that, much like a pebble dropped into a pond causing waves to ripple outwards touching everything in the pond, you can cause the same ripple effect in your world. The first step is to examine your life pattern; for over time, you have developed these repetitive behaviors in order to deal with life. The problem is these behaviors never solve the dilemma. Over and over, you repeat these activities until they become automatic. So now, when something stresses you, you respond out of habit, much like an addict.

My son-in-law taught people to challenge the problem. Most people don't consider their thinking process. In retrospect, they may think about how they responded and wish they had done something else. The challenge is to think again; challenge your thinking, your pattern. Your greatest enemy is the devil using your self-talk, the things you automatically tell yourself every day, against you.

Most people tend to have at least one or two masks. It's almost as if there are different people inside one body. The problem becomes how do you know which one is the real you–the person whom God created?

Are you the person others see in church, at work, or at home? Are you the smiling person filled with love, compassion, and joy? Are you willing to eagerly help and assist others in a patient, caring manner? Perhaps you are the person you've become when you're alone and no one else is around – depressed, negative, and tired. It doesn't matter what your vocation is, you still need to discover the real you. Perhaps you are the life of the party, adept in your profession and intellect, but then make wrong choices or do the wrong things for the right reasons.

There are two kinds of you: The original you and the one you created. If there is a gap between the two personalities, it's time for a change.

The problem is how do you maintain who you are, no matter where you are? Pray and ask God to help you figure out who the real you is. If you maintain a job around others, you obviously have people skills and social skills. Try to develop those gifts, no matter if you are at home, work, or church. Don't try to please others just to earn their approval and minimize the impression you make. You may feel too busy or overwhelmed to evaluate properly the good things in your life. Ask yourself, "Am I busy following God's Will or am I wrapped up in doing things so others will notice and praise me?"

Busyness can become a defense mechanism to avoid intimacy. There were times when David found it difficult to take his own advice. If he had clients in his office and was counseling them about their behavior, immediately, he would insist on writing a treatment plan that would eliminate half of their activities and reprioritize their lives. Yet, he felt like he didn't have the time to do that for himself.

There is nothing quite as humbling and simultaneously wonderful as when a mother gains wisdom from her children. I certainly gained a wealth of knowledge and spiritual impartation from my son-in-law, David. He taught me how to soothe my mind and open doors that I had closed in the past. He encouraged me to think about what God wanted for me.

After meditating on His Word, God helped me to identify the things that were distracting me. Most people think of drugs, alcohol, or gambling when they hear the word addiction. The definition, however, says, "Addiction is the state of being enslaved to an object or way of thinking that's psychologically or physically habit-forming to the extent that its cessation causes severe trauma."

Spiritually, an addiction is living in a darkened place losing your sensitivity to God. Ephesians 4:18-19 states, "Having the understanding darkened, being alienated from the life of God through the ignorance that is in them, because of the blindness of their heart: Who being past feeling have given themselves over unto lasciviousness, to work all uncleanness with greediness."

Simply put, it means to indulge in impurity with a constant lust for more. People can be addicted to substances, relationships, and behaviors.

Top Addictions

Alcohol	Food
Video Games	Work
Crime	Pornography
Pain	Exercise
Sex	Caffeine
Internet	Gambling
Cutting	Drugs
Eating	Stealing
Marijuana	People-pleasing

David and Shawnie actually worked for a community corrections facility and helped rehabilitate many members of the community. They have counseled hundreds of people living with addictions. Likewise, we have travelled as a team to minister to others in the churches who struggle with addictions, which is a cruel master that leads to destruction.

We brought the message of the love of God who delights in healing and delivers them from their potential destruction and demise. Psalm 107:20 promises, "He sent His word, and healed them, and delivered them from their destructions."

It's important to speak to God and to listen for Him to reply. Remember that God is here for a reason. He yearns to interact with you on a regular basis through fellowship, Bible study, prayer, and times of quietness.

You cannot solve your problems until you first identify what needs resolving. Be brutally honest with yourself. It's quite possible you have believed the lies without realizing it. Write out the issues you have, and then write out the ways you need to refocus on making positive affirmations instead of repeating the same lies. For every lie you hear about yourself, replace it with a truth. For example, one lie you might tell yourself is, "I'm a terrible person, and no one loves me." As soon as you start to repeat that lie, make the choice to replace it with the truth, "I'm a precious child of God, made in His image, and Jesus loves me so much that He died a horrific death so that I might be saved."

Once you realize the goals God intends for you, start making an active plan to obtain those goals.

Instead of focusing on your negative attributes or weaknesses, replace them with positive ones and identify your strengths.

Once again, don't forget to set aside several times each day to pray. During those times, make sure you thank God for your blessings. Once you start actively looking for them, you'll soon discover God has been showering you with blessings every single day.

A TIME TO REFLECT:

1. What has prevented you from changing?

    _____

    _____

    _____

    _____

    _____

2. What are you addicted to and why are these things important to you?

    _____

    _____

    _____

    _____

    _____

3. What injustices in the world bother you?

    _____

    _____

    _____

    _____

    _____

_____

_____

4. What can you do to change those injustices?

_____

_____

_____

_____

_____

_____

5. What lies do you tell yourself in order to
   feed your addictions?

_____

_____

_____

_____

_____

_____

_____

REPEAT THE RESOLUTION:

I resolve to choose to be the original, unique, real me.

CHAPTER 8
CHALLENGED TO CHANGE:
FROM IMMATURITY TO MATURITY

It's time to change. Yes, God is challenging you to alter your life. Respond to the challenge by making a permanent change regarding the way you think. If God has given you multiple gifts and talents, it's imperative to know what He is assigning you to do at this specific time in your life.

There is a season when God calls you to switch to another frequency or change the channel. Something is shifting within your spirit.

God spoke to me through the song, "I Will Change Your Name," by D.J. Butler. He sings about how God is able to take broken people and change them. In doing so, He also changes the people's names. If you have ever been called lazy, stupid, or an outsider, then you can appreciate how God can change your name to precious, child, and beloved.

When I decided to follow Jesus, I didn't realize that I was surrendering my life to a total commitment. Jesus' mission became my mission, and I accepted the challenge to a lifetime transformation.

When I heard that sweet, loving voice of God directing me to write *Challenged to Change*, I was relieved. Many other distractions were placed in their proper perspectives, and I was able to focus. This chapter is a revised version of a message that God anointed me to preach over eight years ago.

In the past, God had assigned me to minister to those who had experienced childhood injuries, challenges, abuses, and losses that rendered them helpless.

Unbeknownst to me, it was time to pass the ministry baton to others in order for me to experience another transition that God had planned for me. God shifted my assignment from mentoring numerous women to coaching others by encouraging them to write self-published books.

Pastor C. Shawn Tyson told me, "Now is the time. Your assignment will shift, and the Internet will be one of the tools you will use to bless others."

This shift in ministry reduced my stress levels and decreased the need for me to travel while also affecting more people. God strategically grants the wisdom for one to be a disciple in the church and community and to be able to provide opportunities, allowing others to rise above their negativity, to equip them to dream again, and see visions of their abundant lives.

Now, others can hear my voice through my writing, and God uses my words to develop perception, perspective, and attitude in the spirit, soul, and body. The ministry mission never changes, but the methods used should change with the times.

Teamwork is a crucial method during today's information age in leadership and development. Learning ministry methods during this time is crucial to bridge the generation gap, as well as your continued education to improve your quality and abilities in life. Leaders are readers.

Statistics state that fewer Americans are reading books today; yet, I dare to take another risk and fulfill a great desire to publish a "New York Times Best Seller." I am a leader living off of my "bucket list" and have several years to leave a legacy to millions who desire to live a better life.

Many friends encouraged me to reread the books that I have written, which are cathartic. I was absolutely astounded when I received thousands of letters from readers in prisons, churches of all denominations, males, females, all socio-economic statuses, races, countries, and readers from the ages of eight to eighty.

My friend, Roderick Preston, recently shared with me that a powerful woman of God posted on Facebook that she received a book in Hawaii, seven years ago, that changed her life. I greatly anticipated learning who the author was who helped her change her life. Roderick said, "Guess who the author is." Oblivious to what should have perhaps been the obvious, I chuckled when he answered, "Cheryl Bass-Foster, author of *From Pain to Power*."

Some readers were encouraged, while others were inspired and motivated to move on to better relationships; several changed, and many were led to salvation. It's always been my desire to write a compilation of all the books that God led me to write during my transformation process. However, the eight years of obscurity hidden in sickness presented challenges.

I knew this was another clarion call from God to publish the next phase of my developmental transformation. I took intentional steps toward being transformed. Tested, tried and being marinated in His words was challenging, but I suffered so it would be palatable and easier for you to change.

CHALLENGED TO CHANGE:

Challenge is defined as major threats and actions that impact one's well-being, the very survival of the existing system. Change would be the response or choice to move from a range of extreme immaturity to extreme maturity.

Challenge means to fight resistance and to answer and explain. The definition of change is to be transformed or to cross forms from natural to spiritual. The *Challenged to Change* theme is to fight resistance in the direction you were going and answer or explain to God why it's been difficult for you to cross from natural to spiritual beings and renew your mind; and then repent and turn in His direction. The crux of God's message to you is that some changes require new choices and decisions; others do not make choices; choices are made for them; change can occur from tragedies, crises, doors of opportunity, seasons, or deaths.

What you have attempted to change in the past shall supernaturally transcend you in the next year. Read Deuteronomy chapters six and seven, which identify that you have crossed into prosperity, the land that flows with milk and honey. You may have enemies (the inner you) that you've had to evict off your premises.

You have just crossed over into the Promised Land to possess houses that you didn't build and are living in a prosperous land, not because you've been obedient or worthy. If you really examine your relationship with God, it's likely that you'll discover that you've been stiff-necked, discouraged, and disobedient, but God said, "But I promised." He also warns about disobedience and the consequences. This is not the time to return to your nature from the fall, but to progress on the journey to the Promised Land.

Change is beneficial; yet, human nature has two ways to resist change:

1. Loyalty to habits, attitudes, or behaviors.

2. Failure to yield completely to learn new information.

It is often difficult for Christians to adapt to unfamiliar changes that are different from the fundamental structure they have become comfortable with. The structure provides a safety net, and the change demands great discipline. When presented with the opportunity for a beneficial change that involves risk, Christians can miss opportunities as a result of the lack of knowledge, out of ignorance, and resort to hearsay as reliable sources of truth.

PICTURE THIS

Picture an array of newly-transformed, beautiful butterflies; however, sitting in the midst of them is one, gray, dull, wingless caterpillar stating, "I don't care how good the rest of you feel, I ain't changing."

Change may be one of the hardest things you ever attempt to do. Change requires that you become different, returning to the original creature you were created to be, and not the imposter.

Jesus is the majestic model, overcoming emotions during challenges and human experiences. Simon Peter is the object lesson on how to change during seasons of challenge. When Jesus calls your name, you have to change. You are more than a conqueror, and, just like butterflies, it's impossible to return to a lesser state when we are truly transformed.

Simon Peter, a disciple of Jesus, is a perfect example of how faith evolves when Jesus calls your name. The first time that Jesus speaks to Simon Peter (Simon is his Jewish name and Peter is his Christian name) occurs when Jesus is walking along Galilee's shore and spots the two brothers, Simon and Andrew, fishing. "Follow me and I'll make you fishers of men."

After Jesus is crucified and resurrected, He speaks to Peter once more. "Peter do you love me?" The three years in between those words is a season of change for Simon Peter. Not only did his name change from Simon to Peter, but also Peter overcame many challenges.

Follow me are two words that posed several challenges, yet enabled Simon Peter to live through a transition and transformation. When Simon stepped beyond his comfort zone and changed his occupation from fisherman to disciple, he inherited a calling, a promise, an identity, and a destiny.

This same process enables you to observe a mixture of conditional and unconditional promises regarding predictable challenges that determine whether you will choose to follow destiny and change or remain as you are and regress.

When Jesus entered Simon's life, Simon lived a life of contradictions. He was impulsive, slow to see the truth, insecure, and fearful. At the same time, he was courageous, self-sacrificing, loving, humble, and beautiful because Jesus made it all possible.

Simon's challenge to change was based upon choices. He and Andrew, his brother, immediately dropped their nets as fishermen and left their old identity. When Simon attempted to face a challenge based on his emotions, he failed. When he faced a challenge based upon what Jesus said, he succeeded.

In Mark 1:17, Jesus called out to Simon, and Simon made the choice to follow Jesus. He obeyed Jesus. In contrast, the verse Matthew 14:29 shows how Peter allowed his fear to get the better of him. He saw Jesus on the sea, walking on the water. Jesus commanded Peter to come to him. At first, Peter did manage to step on the water, but as soon as the wind started blowing, Peter became frightened and distracted and cried out, "Lord, save me!"

Later, in Matthew 16:15-17, Jesus asks Peter, "Who do you say I am?"

Immediately Peter answers, "You are the Messiah, the Son of the living God."

Jesus blesses Peter for his faithfulness and confidence. Just before Jesus' death, in John 13:36, we see Peter questioning Jesus. "Where are you going?"

Jesus answered, "Where I am going, you cannot follow."

Peter is almost boastful in his answer. "Lord, why can't I follow you now? I'll lay down my life for you." However, Jesus knew that Peter would deny him three times before the rooster crowed.

Lastly, in John 21:15-19, Jesus asks Peter three times if he loves Him. Peter felt hurt that Jesus questioned him. Jesus finally replies, "Follow me."

After examining these passages, it's easy to wonder how Peter could be so anointed, yet at the same time, so immature. Did he still have an identity crisis after walking with Jesus for three years? Jesus knew that Simon's identity perhaps lay in his ability to catch fish. When Simon lived by the promises and revelations of Jesus, he lived in a higher identity, the original intentions of God.

How could someone so courageous be so cowardly; wise, yet, foolish? Although if you are honest with yourself, it's possible that others could say the same thing about you. In spite of Simon's weaknesses, Jesus changed Simon's name, which means reeds, to Peter, which means rock. When God changes a person's name, He changes his statue. In Matthew 16:18, Jesus stated, "Upon this rock I will build my church."

Many people believe that this statement means the Church would be built upon a foundation of prophets and apostles with Jesus being the cornerstone of the Church (1 Peter 2). Jesus knows your strengths and weaknesses, but allows you to discover them to see what's really in your heart. Simon failed because of his pride. He wanted to be in control. Simon Peter had a preconceived idea of what the Christian walk should be. It's impossible to know what you might do given the circumstances. Until you actually experience something, you can only assume that you would act one way or another. You should never assume that your journey is over because only God knows when that time will be.

Even though he followed Jesus for a season, he never stopped being Simon. He walked in self-confidence, self-righteousness, and pride. Jesus continually challenged Simon's old habits, attitudes, behaviors, and preconceived concepts about Christian discipleship.

Simon felt he must present a perfect image based upon his performance; and Jesus sought people who needed His help on a daily basis so He could heal them with His unconditional love and send them out to be witnesses with a testimony conveying love to others.

Even though Peter failed, he never failed to follow Jesus. "The steps of a good man are ordained by the Lord: and he delights in his way. Though he fell, he shall not be utterly cast down: for the Lord upholds him with His hand" (Psalms 37:23-24).

As you follow Jesus and continue in His presence, He will show you which choices you should make, and you will become the person you were born to be and do what you were born to do.

Simon eventually dies out to his old sin-dominated man united with the old Adam. He also had to do some thorough dying out to who he thought himself to be. Until he died to the old inner vision of himself, the core beliefs of Christ's words continued to come to him as a personal shock.

When Simon Peter was between a rock and a hard place, he returned to his old, natural, human desires and behaviors. He went fishing. Anyone who desires to be a follower of Jesus Christ must die out to self and leave self in the grave. Jesus, with His unconditional love, perceives that Simon Peter had failed to see who he really was and challenged him three times, once for each time he denied Jesus Christ. Peter denied Jesus at the most crucial time in His life, when He needed him the most.

KEYS TO CHANGE

Three days earlier at a campfire, Simon had denied three times that he ever knew Jesus. With these denials, Simon Peter was symbolically crucified and killed as he experienced failure. Later, at another camp, Jesus symbolically resurrected Simon Peter when Jesus asked him three times, "Do you love me?" Finally, after all the brutal sifting and failure, Peter answered the three questions.

Jesus asked Peter, "Do you love me more than these, the other disciples, fishing, your self-interest?"

Peter answered, "Yes, I love you."

Jesus encouraged him to focus on his calling rather than his occupation of fisherman. "Feed my lambs."

The second time Jesus asked, "Peter, do you love me?"

Peter responded, "Yea Lord, you know that I love you."

In English, we use only one word for love. The first two times that Jesus asked Peter if he loved Him, He used the Greek word, *agape*, which refers to the unconditional type of love. When Peter answered, he used the word, *phileo*, which is more like a brotherly love. The third time both Jesus and Peter used the term, *phileo*.

Jesus asked this question three times because He wanted to stress that Peter now had a new role in life. Jesus commanded Peter, "Feed my sheep." He promoted Peter, and Peter was transformed.

Peter's power to change depended on his ability to direct and manage his emotions. He learned how to give and to receive divine love; love is not an emotion, but a commitment. Peter offered himself completely to Jesus. Renewing his mind rendered his soul in the control of Jesus. He stripped his mind down and chose to receive a majestic memory. He renounced his past memories and actions. According to Romans 12:2, Peter is in position to prove the acceptable and perfect Will of God by prayer and imagination. Prayer creates while the word changes. He was consumed by the Word of God.

I challenge you to change. Remember, Jesus prayed that your faith will not fail you. Prayer changed me.

I took the "90-Day Mental Fitness Challenge" with the specific intention of identifying my hidden areas that challenged me from becoming a great leader for God. It was by far one of the greatest investments I've ever made for myself. After completing the course, God revealed one of my weaknesses was my attitude. Enlightened, I sought God diligently to heal what He revealed with the results of the test. God had been yelling in my ear for years. "Stop, look, and listen to your life." I found it easy to tell others this, but had a difficult time following my own advice.

My three strengths were character, finances, and legacy while my three weaknesses were attitude, adversity, and conflict resolution. As a counselor, minister, and compassionate person, I didn't believe it. However, the test results don't lie. It was time for me to put on my Christian work clothes and work on my own soul salvation. I felt shock and disbelief at first. My apathy and excuses had left an undefined pain in my heart. God's love allowed me to stretch and transition. It's not easy to see what others can see in you. But by the grace of God, He will show you your blind spots.

The imposter in me hid behind depression. In Psalm 42:5 the author asks, "Why art thou cast down, O my soul? and why art thou disquieted in me? hope thou in God: for I shall yet praise him for the help of his countenance." This mentality can cause people to feel unbalanced and uncoordinated. Your mind seeks to explain, create, and control. Your body seeks to experience, accomplish, and grow. Your heart seeks to attach, give, and feel. By examining your inner dialog, it will reveal what type of relationship you have with yourself.

It is not a sin to be depressed. It is a sin if you forget that you have hope in God and fail to encourage yourself. II Corinthians 7:6 states, "God comforts those who are cast down." I learned how to walk through depression by continuing to tell myself the truth: *It's true that I'm feeling bad. It's unpleasant; however, it is manageable. It may take time to overcome depression. Your natural reactions may cause spiritual problems. You must decide to come out of depression, loneliness, and fear.*

The Spirit of God never leaves you alone in your depression. The most damaging lies are the ones that you tell yourself. If you believe those lies, it will only feed the depression and continue the vicious cycle.

I overcame depression by returning to doing what I am meant to do. I learned the value of boundaries, and I have resisted the urge to get overly involved in the lives of others.

Galatians 6:1-5 gives excellent advice. "Brethren, if a man be overtaken in a fault, ye which are spiritual, restore such a one in the spirit of meekness; considering thyself, lest thou also be tempted. Bear ye one another's burdens, and so fulfil the law of Christ. For if a man think himself to be something, when he is nothing, he deceiveth himself. But let every man prove his own work, and then shall he have rejoicing in himself alone, and not in another. For every man shall bear his own burden."

Simply said, you should help others carry their burdens until they are strong enough and are able to carry their own burden. My role is limited to teaching others life skills to live by and bringing them to Jesus. I cannot heal them; that is up to God.

A TIME TO REFLECT:

1. What names do you call yourself?

   _____

   _____

   _____

   _____

   _____

2. What gifts has God given you?

   _____

   _____

   _____

   _____

3. How do you use those gifts?

   _____

   _____

   _____

   _____

   _____

4. In what ways have you been resisting change?

_____

_____

_____

_____

_____

_____

5. When and how have you denied Jesus?

_____

_____

_____

_____

6. What type of a relationship do you have with yourself?

_____

_____

_____

_____

_____

7. What do you fish for during times of stress?

_____

_____

_____

_____

_____

REPEAT THE RESOLUTION:

I resolve to overcome resistance to blind spots, but
instead, will face them in order to change.

CHAPTER 9

CHALLENGED TO CHANGE WHEN GOD REVEALS TO HEAL: FLIP THE SCRIPT

Prayer is vital to the healing process. Prayer creates the opportunity to change and the Word changes you. Do you accept the change to pray and prepare for the manifestation of the promises of God?

When Simon Peter was called by Jesus, he inherited a calling, a promise, an identity, and God. Immediately, he came under the attack of the enemy to defy what God had ordained.

Jesus prayed for Simon Peter in St. Luke 22:31-32, "And the Lord said, 'Simon, Simon, behold, Satan hath desired to have you, that he may sift you as wheat: but I have prayed that thy faith fail thee not: and when thou art converted, strengthen thy brethren.'"

Jesus also prays that your faith will lead you through a tedious process when you become weary and feel faint.

When Jesus changed Simon's name to Peter, He changed his nature. He offers you the same promise.

His specific intent is to change your name, nature, character, and relationship with God in divine authority.

After Jesus prayed for Simon Peter, He modeled how to pray in the Garden of Gethsemane during His challenge. Jesus was isolated in a dark place by divine design.

Isolation can give you a desire to break all of your limitations so that you can deal with any situation.

Apostle Peter, Pastor of The Jesus Pentecostal Church, manifested many miracles and glorified God. In Acts, when Peter and John were on their way to the temple, they encountered a lame man who was begging for money while sitting at the Gate Beautiful. Peter knew the keys of authority were given to him, and he commanded the man to look on them.

He replied, "Silver and gold have I none, but such that I have I give unto thee." Peter had the power of prophetic authority for miracles and healings in a voice-activated kingdom. Prophecies must contain encouragement, identification, gifts, blessings, and favorable conditions.

Peter was authorized to speak in the name of Jesus. Victims don't have the power to speak for themselves; therefore, another person has to speak for them. Once the victim jumped up and leaped, he and others were looking at Peter and John in amazement.

It is not your faith that brings about healing and miracles but your faith in God. The process of transitioning and transforming while learning how to pray, praise, and worship God empowers you.

As a newborn believer, God works for you. He is gracious by allowing time together in prayer to actually listen to you moan and weep, begging Him to change broken relationships, finances, and health.

Prayer, at the newborn stage, allows you to be dependent upon God for everything. He does answer your prayers immediately to develop a trusting relationship, building your foundation of faith in God. Prayer is a refreshing time to release your heart of daunting pains and traumatic memories.

During my spiritual immaturity, I cried about everything while at Jesus' feet. I worried about everything and rehearsed all negative occurrences. I cried every day for two years, but I didn't realize that God was using those tears as a way to heal me until six years later on Sunday, February 16, 2014. God revealed through my pastor, Suffragan Bishop C. Shawn Tyson's message, "The Believer's Confidence," that tears are cleansing agents for change.

Pain is a purifying agent, and the tears were cleansing toxins, residues, and imperfections. Prayer breaks up the unplanted ground of our hearts and allows God to plant seeds of love and light, even while we are underground in darkness. The

Bible states that all hearts are deceitful and desperately wicked, yet once the hardness and malice is broken up in your heart, then God can give you a spiritual bypass and begin to heal you.

The angry tears shed during heartbreaks transform into liquid tears before God in the right season, and at the right time, He uses them to water His promises that will break through in due season. Liquid tears that once watered your seeds now turn into showers of blessings in God's sight. He uses the prayers and is touched by your infirmities, and discerns the personality quirks in your unconscious and subconscious mind so you can be free to live in the conscious presence daily.

Prayer is the process by which you become aware of your inabilities and your need for His great ability. When you go through this process, you will stop asking why bad things happen to good people and realize your righteousness is as filthy rags.

At the end of the process, outside circumstances will no longer control you. Prayer creates while God's Word changes you. Prayer breaks the interpersonal barriers to progress. These inner barriers are part of life, and maturity develops after struggling with such inner workings.

Prayer heals wounded, heartbroken, and down and out Christians and spiritually cleanses your wounds. God uses prayer to build character.

When my heart felt broken after my divorce, God used specific intentional prayers regarding forgiveness to heal me. The Bible is full of such promises from God. The following are just two of the many examples God provides for you in His Word: "He healeth the broken in heart, and bindeth up their wounds" (Psalm 147:3); "The LORD [is] nigh unto them that are of a broken heart; and saveth such as be of a contrite spirit" (Psalm 34:18).

When looking for love in all the wrong places, God revealed that I had to live with the consequences of my wrong choices. I had looked for so-called bad boys because I was curious about a different lifestyle other than the nice girl from the middle class.

Therefore, when Benny Bass and I were courting, I made him my god and denied his faults. Our glows and giddy outward appearance was because this courtship provided a temporary nurturing. We actually regressed to an earlier stage of development.

Once we were married, I fought for the affection that was promised in courtship, only to discover that he couldn't provide for my needs nor could I fulfill his because of our own deficiencies. Yet, I continued to go through life looking for a parent. Looking for love in the wrong places prevented me from seeing the love of God.

Dating in holiness is different than secular dating. I had to value myself before I could expect anyone else to respect me. I learned tough love and the original intention for sacred marriages. Luther and I were married on November 16th, 1991.

This marriage was now sacred and consummated on our honeymoon. Our marriage is a spiritual assignment to improve the quality of one another. I learned how to receive love from Luther

Foster. He is the best husband, hand-picked by God for me. He is a man who loves God; therefore, he is able to love me much like Christ loves the church. We support one another by interceding for one another.

Prayer will lead and guide you to your soulmate, predesigned for you before the foundation of the world. Marriage transcends us through a process of becoming one; therefore, it's not just obtaining the promise, but it's the process of self-disclosure.

Being married to Luther has given me the incentive to heal old wounds. When pain is triggered, my husband is in a position to minister to me, and I to him.

As you heal, many of your present relationships will seem to change and become less attractive. That's why it is important to keep your marriage fresh and interesting with mysteries that God unfolds to do some unique activities together.

It is imperative for a family to grow together and discover the truth of Jesus. I watched Pastor

Wagner use wisdom and timing in maintaining growth and maturity, and today, I am blessed that Luther was my caregiver for eight years. We grew closer, and he was elevated as I was still and quiet. God is a wonder.

Prayer illuminates things that you don't understand. God gives answers to prayers; solutions to problems; understanding to revelation; and manifestation to promises.

After studying St. Matthew 6:24-34, I discovered that I needed to establish priorities that would motivate me.

Whatever choices you make, if you are in agreement with the Will of God, it will result in righteousness and a pure heart.

Worry never resolves anything. It actually blocks solutions from coming to you. To worry is to fill your mind with negative thoughts. It is like praying, but in a negative way. Studies show that over ninety percent of what people worry about never happens.

Worry was sapping the life out of me and stripping my vitality. Adversity is the result of the incorrect use of our thoughts. "As a man thinketh in his heart so is he" (Proverbs 23:7).

Worry means to strangle, choke the life out of you, or causes you to be afflicted with mental distress or agitation. An extreme form of worry is anxiety, which is the distress of the mind, which is a sin.

The subconscious fears and negative thoughts can choke your faith, bind your joy, and hinder your personal relationship with the Lord.

Worry can also cause feelings of unworthiness. I often wondered why God wouldn't release me from my challenges. Now, I know that He loved me too much to leave me in that state. He used my adversities to introduce me to myself.

The gifts that God has given you are not dependent upon the reactions of others.

As an adolescent believer maturing in God, He works in you as you experience movements in transition from the newborn stage. During the adolescent stage, it's no longer about you, but you begin to comprehend, grasp, and interpret the times and seasons of God's Will. Specific intent is based on what is important to God. Pray His thoughts and obey His commands.

Very few rebellious adolescents want to obey authority figures. Teens often think they know what's right for them. Most are stuck in this struggle now. Many people are adults with adolescent mindsets. Psalm 131:2 states, "Surely I have behaved and quieted myself, as a child that is weaned of his mother: my soul is even as a weaned child." God wants you to discard many learned, outdated patterns of behavior that you used to protect yourself as a child. I Corinthians 13:11 admonishes you to put away childish things.

During this season, there is more self-disclosure identifying the voided places that need to be recreated during this Dispensation of Grace. The Dispensation of Grace often is referred to as the era after Christ died on the cross. It's the time when the first churches formed and spread out to tell as many people as possible about the wonderful news of Jesus. We are living in a space of grace to discover who we are and learn and develop the proper skillsets.

We also learn the proper respect and acknowledge that we desire to thank God by giving Him praise.

You must embrace the retooling, reframing, and renewing God offers you. Numbers 23:19 states, "God is not a man, that he should lie; neither the son of man, that he should repent: hath he said, and shall he not do it? or hath he spoken, and shall he not make it good?" This verse should reassure you that God doesn't lie to you. When He says He will do something, it will be done. It may not always happen when you want it, but it will occur according to God's timetable. Although God doesn't lie to you, perhaps there are times when you have not only lied to God, but also to yourself.

As related to God, you have two kinds of E.G.O.s. The first represents you **E**dging **G**od **O**ut. While you mature, God fills in the gaps, so now

E.G.O. stands for **E**xalting **G**od **O**nly. Fear-based thoughts are embedded in your mind. These are the lies you have told yourself or that others have said about you until you believed them to be true. Faith-based thoughts are the truths that God created in your spiritual DNA. II Corinthians 5:17 states, "Therefore, if any man be in Christ, he is a new creature: old things are passed away; behold, all things are become new." You have a new nature; you are a new creature. You have the ability to renew your mind. As a born-again believer, you have received innate powers to change from the inside out.

God opened the windows to heal the injured grooves in my brain, like a needle stuck on a scratched record. It remains stuck in that groove until the needle is moved to another place.

God heals as He reveals your blind spots because salvation is an event, but sanctification is a process that will continually deliver, develop, and enable you to use your gifts to build up the people you encounter.

As you look through the windows of your heart, you can see Christ inside you. You also can hear Him, and are able to open the door of your heart so He can commune with you on a regular basis. You are now challenged to lift your vision, to open your eyes, to reveal the Truth, to bring in Life and Light, which will enable you to let go of misconceptions. Light is not always welcome when it first shines into darkness because your eyes are not accustomed to it.

However, the Light that shines through these windows is necessary in order to see the truth. You want God to heal you from spiritual blindness.

You will continue to make spiritual progress if you have the spiritual vision of Jesus Christ. Vision is essential to progress. Spiritual sight is something that happens on the inside when your inner spiritual eyes have been opened.

While I was in the midst of my progress to a permanent change, I was still stuck in the area of discipline. God told me the truth. I truly believed that my being chronically nice to everyone was spiritual compassion, but I soon learned it was just another type of addiction.

God opened the windows of opportunity so I could see me. Prayer opened the window and restored my original devotion, dedication, desire, discernment to live beyond dead things, directions, and divine miracles.

As an adult, God works through you, and your conversations with Him should be faith-based, hopeful, trusting, and pure. You now will respond with acceptance instead of manipulation. Praying in the supernatural realm develops your ability to write the visions of God, listen to what He is downloading, and decode the spiritual Morse Code used in battle to confront and confuse demonic imps.

When you pray, begin by entering into the spiritual realm. When you kneel down to pray, you are about to leave your body and enter the spirit realm. Be aware in the spirit realm; there are always demonic spirits, dead spirits, and angelic spirits.

First, go to God, get His Will, and ask for His permission to perform any task He gives you. Now, you can instruct angels and cast out devils. You can pray, "I submit myself under your authority. As you rule on this earth, so will I. May I ascend to Heaven to receive Your plan, and descend to Earth to put the plan in operation."

In prayer, God sends angels to enter the throne room, but when you praise and worship Him, He comes Himself. The God of Glory comes for the praise. God is searching Earth for clean vessels.

Prayer is the communication system designed by God for people to communicate with God. Prayer has codes to get you out of the flesh and into the Spirit to communicate with God. It is at this point that you have reached Heaven, and Heaven is conveying commands for earthly operation. The key element of prayer is to bring the Kingdom of God to Earth. Matthew 6:10 states, "Thy kingdom come, thy will be done."

Prayer identifies which Kingdom needs to be addressed on a given day: The Kingdom of God;

The Kingdom of Heaven; The Kingdom of Man; or The Kingdom of Hell.

Prayer sends the spirit to find the infirmity underground to heal your personality quirks. Prayer is the process by which you come into awareness of your inabilities and your need for His great ability. Prayer actually reveals the triggers to carnal behavior. According to many support groups, general triggers occur for most people when they are hungry, angry, lonely, or tired. The acronym H.A.L.T. is used to remind people not to make major decisions during these times. They may regress to a painful memory and act it out. When you go through this process, you will stop asking why bad things happen to good people and realize your righteousness is as filthy rags and but for the grace of God, there go I. I believe a hidden infirmity in addictions is an epidemic today during a time of people searching for more meaningful lives and levels of living. There is apathy in the atmosphere that stifles, smothers, and chokes the living daylight out of you if you are not careful.

Problem: The inability to get pleasure out of normal things in life is an extreme form of depression and can be seen in Post-Traumatic Stress Disorders. This occurs when you abuse the pleasure center of the brain for your own excitement. This can rob one of the original purpose of the pleasure. Boredom is the major symptom.

Solution: God put the pleasure system in your brain to experience the pleasure of God. It is God's pleasure to return creativity and imagination for the source of entertainment.

Prayer must return to the homes, school systems, public and political institutions, religious sects, and the Church.

"And rising very early in the morning, while it was still dark, he (Jesus) departed and went out to a desolate place, and there he prayed." St. Mark 1:35

Pastor Tyson shared that scripture and profound principles with me during our 5:00 AM. Ministry of Prayer And Intercession.

"1. Prayer stabilizes our mind and keeps our mind focused upon God.

2. We will transform our spirits and minds from anxiety and self-reliance to a disposition of humility and confidence in God. Read Philippians 4.
3. The Word of God will not open its mysteries to us without prayer.

Where you place your mind at the beginning of the day will determine where you park your mind at the end of the day."

A TIME TO REFLECT:

1. What names have you been called in the past?

   _____

   _____

   _____

2. What names do you believe Jesus uses for you?

   _____

   _____

   _____

3. What are your needs that you know God has taken care of?

   _____

   _____

   _____

   _____

4. What places in your life do you look for love?

   _____

   _____

_____

_____

5. What relationships do you need to change or
   get out of and why?

   _____

   _____

   _____

   _____

   _____

6. What worries do you have today that you
   need to hand over to God?

   _____

   _____

   _____

REPEAT THE RESOLUTION:

I resolve to pray daily to develop an intimate
relationship with God. He reveals to heal.

CHAPTER 10

CHALLENGED TO CHANGE WHEN WINDOWS OF OPPORTUNITY OPEN: SEE JESUS

As a victorious leader, I can lead others from rock bottom to a place of hope–the Rock. Because of God's grace, I have enough faith to love and forgive; forgiveness is the final form of love.

I had the wrong perception of my qualities, posture, position, and my disability. I didn't fear the judgment of others; I feared my own judgment. However, I repented and used my disability to be a messenger of hope and possibility for others. I am only an example that proves you, too, can overcome challenges.

I am a transformed witness and testify that with God, all things are possible. Yes, I am transforming daily from the caterpillar, which just left the cocoon hanging upside down in the dark, broke through that threadlike bondage, and now sits alone with wet wings. Most days, I sit alone because no one can touch my wet wings, because strengthening them requires waiting on the drying process. In order to make a successful transformation from a victim to a leader, it was essential that the old me died out before I could fully realize the glory of the new life. There had to be a period of isolation in which I received my assignment from God. Only then can a butterfly spread its wings, and delicately but powerfully affect life by flying from person to person, pollinating the population with the love of Christ.

I am eternally grateful for having a first-hand experience of the depths of human pain and the excruciating, mind-boggling effect that pain has on the human mind. I am privileged to know how important it is to be equipped and skilled to minister to people suffering from stress and mental illnesses. Today, I am empowered, and I realize that there are countless souls crying, "Stop the judgment, and help me heal."

Everyone in life is eventually *Challenged to Change*. These changes are often preceded by chaos and crisis, which ushers you into a process or perpetual journey. There are many words to represent *change*. They include metamorphosis, transform, restore, regenerate, revive, renew, and repent. The Greek word for repent, *metanoeo,* means, "To think differently."

The implication here is that your behavior is based on your faulty thinking, and change makes you think differently, ushering you into sound-thinking patterns. Hence, God sends chastening trials so that you will repent of ungodly thinking which gives rise to your sinful ways during life's setbacks. When you go through your trials with the right attitude, you grow, learn, and change because of them. King David testifies in Psalm 119:71, "It is good for me that I have been afflicted; that I might learn thy statutes." You go through great trials so that others might benefit from the positive transformation you have experienced.

As the seasons change, it can be natural to think about the life cycle and how all things eventually pass away in order to make room for the springing forth of new life. During this time, the beautiful butterfly symbolizes renewal more than any other creature on earth. The butterfly makes a transformation from an unattractive caterpillar in a process called *metamorphosis*. Before she is transformed, a caterpillar merely lives to eat and grow. In this stage, she may very well become a food source for other creatures. However, if she is given the chance to live, she has so much more potential to offer. After her metamorphosis, the butterfly's new purpose is to pollinate flowers, fruits, and vegetables that produce more seeds to sustain continued life for the human family as well as for the animal kingdom.

As things are natural, so are they spiritual. Through the Father's transformation process, Christians are reborn in Christ Jesus to grow in Him from glory to glory and from strength to strength. As you are changed in Him, you are called to touch others' lives to reproduce more fruitfulness in them. This wonderful cycle continues repeatedly. This is also true for the butterfly effect. The butterfly effect is a metaphor used in chaos theory that describes how one tiny modification can change a multitude of seemingly unrelated things. Some tiny variant such as a butterfly flapping its wings on one side of the world can change the weather in another part of the world. This demonstrates that the tiniest influence on one part of a system can have a huge effect on another part.

Likewise, the human family is a large and complex system, wherein one member's actions or inactions have the potential to influence all others. Our Lord and Savior did not bring us into this reality called *life* to be islands unto ourselves. Like the little butterfly, we have power to influence others, whether positively or negatively. As such, your purpose during and after a personal challenge, like that of the beautifully transformed butterfly, is to add spiritual value to the lives of everyone around you. In order for this to happen, you must die out to the old person called, *self*. This is exactly what the butterfly does. In exchange for a new life of giving, she sheds her old selfish ways of taking.

Yielding to God-ordained challenges promotes newness of life. In turn, a new life lends itself to a new purpose. Jesus *"died for all, that they which live should not henceforth live unto themselves, but unto him which died for them, and rose again. Therefore if any man be in Christ, he is a new creature: old things are passed away; behold, all things are become new"* (2 Corinthians 5:15, 17). It is ironic that death of the old self contributes to new life in Christ. Jesus is the giver of life and all good things that sustain it. It is Jesus' Will that you live life in the overflow, with an abundance of all good things. This truth is declared in John 10:10, *"The thief cometh not, but for to steal, and to kill, and to destroy: I am come that they might have life, and that they might have it more abundantly."* This Scripture represents both good and evil.

When you are covered in the righteousness of God, you are changed in Christ. The hedge that covered Job was the righteousness of God. God's righteousness covers every deficit you have and makes all things new about you (Revelations 21:5). Without God's covering, you are completely exposed.

Because of Job's rapport with God, God had great confidence in him, and this is why God allowed the enemy to tempt him. Job was unaware of the sin of self-righteousness that lived in his heart. The Lord knew the depth of Job's love for Him. Job needed to experience the transforming power of love, and as it is with the butterfly, so it was with Job, Peter, King David, Elijah, you, and me. Job's trials did not destroy his love for God. Instead, it challenged him to change and made him able to pollinate blessings in the lives of others, even in the lives of his wretched friends. Thus, the butterfly effect was at work through everyone's transformation process.

God revealed my identification and location in Him during this process over thirty years ago when He spoke, "You are my butterfly even though you are in your caterpillar stage. You're groping, moping and crawling through life, being stepped on, using temporary legs and supports to keep you from flying. People are grimacing at your present appearance; unbeknownst to them, I make all things beautiful in My time. I beautify the meek with salvation. You can't see the overall picture during this process while you're focused on your personal pain, but there is purpose in your pain."

Today is a new day. On my last birthday, I closed the chapter on that stage of my life. With a joyful, grateful attitude, I am entering into my latter days with a new lease on life. There were times when I never thought I'd survive the transitions in my life. Though the view on emotional illnesses is gradually changing, we still live in a world where many people think of mental illnesses as a stigma, something to be kept behind closed doors. However, God has strengthened me through the process to count it all as joy, because Jesus came that you and I might live an abundant life.

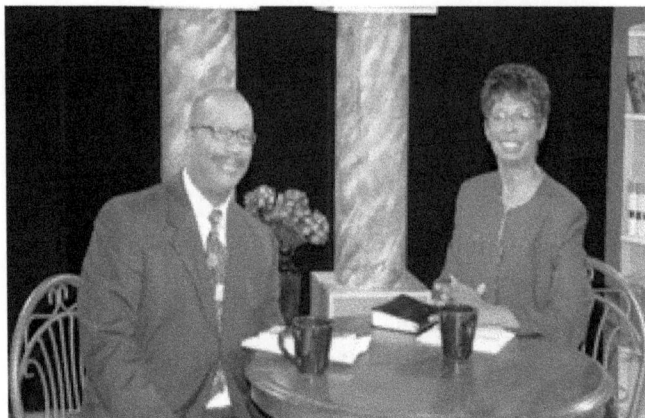

My Story Gives God Glory because He has blessed me to live a victorious life overcoming co-dependency. He does heal the broken in heart and bindeth up our wounds. (Appearance on The Nickol's Worth seated with Dr. Mitch Nickols.)

A TIME TO REFLECT:

1. In what ways am I like a caterpillar?

   _____

   _____

   _____

   _____

   _____

2. What do I need to do to become a butterfly?

   _____

   _____

   _____

   _____

   _____

3. What do I believe is God's plan for the next season of my life?

   _____

   _____

   _____

   _____

   _____

4. What truths about myself do I need to remember when Satan is attacking me?

_____

_____

_____

_____

_____

5. What changes have I made in my attitude since this journey began?

_____

_____

REPEAT THE RESOLUTION:

I resolve to do whatever it takes to live an abundant life with the help of my Lord Jesus Christ. I resolve to accept the challenge to change my attitude and become a beautiful butterfly.

All references have been noted throughout this book, which is written as a testimony to give God Glory.

Any further communication concerning your spiritual growth, personal growth and leadership development may be forwarded to our email addresses:

luthercheryl8@att.net

or

lousphotography888@att.net.

www.ingramcontent.com/pod-product-compliance
Lightning Source LLC
Chambersburg PA
CBHW070346090426
42733CB00009B/1312

www.ingramcontent.com/pod-product-compliance
Lightning Source LLC
Chambersburg PA
CBHW070346090426
42733CB00009B/1303